"Take your time reading this profound book. Jamie Smart is about to blow apart every circumstantial excuse you ever came up with. He's about to put the steering wheel back in your hands."

Garret Kramer, Founder of Inner Sports and Author of *Stillpower*

"The insights you'll get whilst reading *Clarity* will resonant in how you manage day to day but, more importantly, provide a framework for refreshing your priorities, goals and drive."

Peter Lake, Group Business Development Director, JS Group

"The world of leadership, sales and customer engagement has changed radically over the past ten years. People are more savvy, better informed and sick of the same old story. Jamie Smart cuts through the noise of the marketplace and shows you what really works. Profound, practical and instantly applicable; *Clarity* is essential reading if you want to make your mark in the 21st century."

Paul Charmatz, Former Managing Director, Camelot

"Jamie, you really hit the bullseye with this brilliant book; it's a must-read for everyone who wants clarity of mind."

Joe Stumpf, Founder of By Referral Only and Author of *Willing Warrior*

"Jamie Smart takes an outdated paradigm of success and turns it on its head. Pull up a chair, get a copy of *Clarity* and discover how you can experience an exponential increase in clarity and quality of life."

Rich Litvin, co-author of *The Prosperous Coach* and Founder of The Confident Woman's Salon

"Jamie Smart is *brilliant*! In his book *Clarity*, he has unlocked an insight into the real-life matrix. Be ready to have your world turned inside-out because, as Jamie so effortlessly demonstrates, *this* is how it works."

Richard Enion, Dragon's Den Winner, BassToneSlap.com and RichEats.TV

"At last – a book that explains the importance of understanding the nature of thought and how the answers are on the inside! I fully endorse and share Jamie's vision for the 'Thought Revolution'."

Andy Gilbert, Founder & developer of the Go M.A.D.® Thinking System

"Jamie Smart writes in a way that speaks directly to the challenges people face in today's business environment. I'm buying a copy for all my clients."

Cheryl Bond, Ed.D., President, Essential Resilience

"*Clarity* is an amazing book that provides you with the one realization you need to find happiness, wisdom and clarity in life. I highly recommend this book to anyone trying to deal with life stressors and find true wisdom and well-being."

Mark Howard, Ph.D., Clinical Psychologist, ThreePrinciplesInstitute.org

"*Clarity* is an utterly engaging and powerful book that brilliantly elucidates what is undoubtedly *the* most important revolution in psychology. Jamie shares his understanding using a multitude of real-world examples that bring this understanding to life without jargon or hype."

Chantal Burns, Leadership Coach, Teacher
and Consultant, www.ChantalBurns.com

"Jamie Smart has been a master of life change for many years now, but this is an incredible, perhaps the ultimate, expression of his already powerful wisdom. It's quite simply revolutionary."

Alex West, Co-Executive Producer of the original BBC TV series
Who Do You Think You Are?

"This amazing book delivers the single most profound insight deep into your mind. All you have to do is not get in the way!"

Jason Bates, CEO of Freeformers, www.freeformers.com

"This book is the kick up the backside the self-help and success genre so badly needs. A word of warning – this book is very different!"

Simon Hazeldine, Author of *Neuro-Sell*,
International Speaker, Performance Consultant

"If you want real leverage and creativity in your life, read this book."

Catherine Casey M.A., Clinical Psychology,
Principle Based Consultant, San Jose, California

"*Clarity* is awesome. 500 words in and I was on fire and it didn't stop... And what was particularly pleasant was it felt good. Do what every high-performer or entrepreneur looking for modern solutions to live a better life should do: get *Clarity*."

James Lavers, Media Psychologist

"This new understanding not only gave more creativity and success when I was in a good place, it also gives me important insight at other, arguably more important, times. It's massively valuable in my success as modern day businessman."

Julian Freeman, Entrepreneur

"*Clarity* is thought-provoking and profound – a radical and yet common-sense approach to change, leadership and personal development."

Amanda Menahem, HR Director, Hastings Direct

"Brilliant! *Clarity* is packed with inspiration, epiphanies and eurekas on every page. Jamie Smart teaches that clarity is our natural state, and that when we get clear about who we are and about how life works, it helps us to be happier, more successful, and more loving men and women."

Robert Holden Ph.D., Author of *Shift Happens!*,
Authentic Success and *Loveability*

CLARITY

Clear Mind · Better Performance
Bigger Results

Jamie Smart

CAPSTONE

© 2013 Jamie Smart
Innate Thinking® is a registered trademark of Jamie Smart Limited

Registered office
Capstone Publishing Ltd. (A Wiley Company), John Wiley and Sons Ltd, The Atrium, Southern Gate, Chichester, West Sussex, PO19 8SQ, United Kingdom

For details of our global editorial offices, for customer services and for information about how to apply for permission to reuse the copyright material in this book please see our website at www.wiley.com.

The right of the author to be identified as the author of this work has been asserted in accordance with the Copyright, Designs and Patents Act 1988.

Wiley publishes in a variety of print and electronic formats and by print-on-demand. Some material included with standard print versions of this book may not be included in e-books or in print-on-demand. If this book refers to media such as a CD or DVD that is not included in the version you purchased, you may download this material at http://booksupport.wiley.com. For more information about Wiley products, visit www.wiley.com.

Designations used by companies to distinguish their products are often claimed as trademarks. All brand names and product names used in this book and on its cover are trade names, service marks, trademark or registered trademarks of their respective owners. The publisher and the book are not associated with any product or vendor mentioned in this book. None of the companies referenced within the book have endorsed the book.

Limit of Liability/Disclaimer of Warranty: While the publisher and author have used their best efforts in preparing this book, they make no representations or warranties with the respect to the accuracy or completeness of the contents of this book and specifically disclaim any implied warranties of merchantability or fitness for a particular purpose. It is sold on the understanding that the publisher is not engaged in rendering professional services and neither the publisher nor the author shall be liable for damages arising herefrom. If professional advice or other expert assistance is required, the services of a competent professional should be sought.

Library of Congress Cataloging-in-Publication Data is available

A catalogue record for this book is available from the British Library.

ISBN 978-0-857-08448-4 (paperback) ISBN 978-0-857-08445-3 (ebk)
ISBN 978-0-857-08446-0 (ebk) ISBN 978-0-857-08447-7 (ebk)

Set in 10/13pt Sabon by Sparks—www.sparkspublishing.com

Printed in Great Britain by TJ International Ltd, Padstow, Cornwall, UK

Contents

To my daughters,
Matilda and Tallulah

Author's Note

Thomas Kuhn's groundbreaking book, *The Structure of Scientific Revolutions*, introduced the term "paradigm" to describe the prevailing worldview that underpins a scientific field. A paradigm shift – the superseding of such a worldview – is massively disruptive to normal science. Kuhn explained that a new paradigm opens up ways of perceiving and understanding reality that weren't previously available.

Unfortunately, the words "paradigm" and "paradigm shift" have been hijacked by modern marketers, and are used to describe everything from flash-in-the-pan web start-ups to the latest celebrity fad-diet. In reality, the emergence of a new paradigm is a rare and revolutionary phenomenon.

This book includes quotations from a variety of people, ranging from scientists and philosophers to entrepreneurs and media mavens. I've included these quotations because I like them and how they fit with the chapters. However, I am not suggesting that these individuals endorse(d) (or were even aware of) the paradigm this book is pointing to. In fact (except where otherwise noted) I am certain they did not.

It is my assertion that what this book endeavours to describe is a genuinely new paradigm, in the Kuhnian sense. Ironically, it may not meet the scientific criteria for a paradigm as they are currently defined. If my assertion proves to be correct then, in the long term, the criteria may be redefined to include it. Or not. Either way, I invite you to evaluate it in the laboratory of your own life, and decide for yourself.

To your increasing clarity of mind and understanding!

Jamie Smart, 2013

Introduction

"What information consumes is rather obvious: it consumes the attention of its recipients."

Herbert Simon, Economist,
winner of the Nobel Prize
in Economics, 1978

"If a pond is clouded with mud, there's nothing you can do to make the water clear. But when you allow the mud to settle, it will clear on its own, because clarity is the water's natural state..."

Clarity is your *mind's* natural state.

For many years, I've been sharing this simple metaphor in workshops and seminars with business leaders, entrepreneurs, consultants, change-workers and private individuals. As people allow their mud to settle, clarity emerges, and they discover they have what they need for the job at hand.

So what is clarity, and why does it matter? How does clarity work, and why do so many people struggle to find it? Most importantly, how can you find the clarity you need and start benefiting from it?

It's well known that outstanding leaders in every field, from Olympic medal-winners to visionary entrepreneurs, profit from the flow-states that a clear mind brings. With clarity of mind comes the qualities that drive sustainable results. These qualities and results are what individuals and organizations are searching for. But, due to a simple misunderstanding, we've been looking in the wrong place until now.

The purpose of this book is to correct the misunderstanding and help you experience greater and greater clarity, with all the benefits it provides. The book asks and answers the following questions:

1 *What is clarity?* It turns out that clarity is a kind of "universal resource." When we have a clear head, we have everything we need for the job at hand. Ask a nervous speaker what's going through their mind when they're onstage, and they'll explain their fears, worries and anxieties. Ask a confident speaker what they're thinking about onstage and the answer's almost always the same: "Nothing!" This is the case in every field of high performance, from the classroom to the playing field, from the boardroom to the bedroom; when you've got nothing on your mind, you're free to give your best.

2 *Why is clarity essential?* You're going to discover why clarity is so important for living a life that's successful on the *inside* as well as on the outside. You're going to discover that many of the most desirable qualities people struggle to "develop" (such as intuition, resilience, creativity, motivation, confidence and even *leadership*) are actually innate, emergent properties of an uncluttered mind. These drive the results people desire. Clarity is the source of authentic leadership and high performance. It allows us to be present in the moment, and have an enjoyable experience of life. A sense of purpose, direction and entrepreneurial spirit are natural for people with a clear head. So are happiness, freedom, security, love, confidence and peace of mind.

3 *How does clarity work, and how can you get it to work for you?* You're going to be introduced to *Innate Thinking®*, a model of the natural capacity for experience – thinking, feeling and perceiving – that every person is born with. This innate capacity generates 100% of our experience of life, moment to moment.

Clarity is a naturally emergent property of innate thinking – it isn't something you *do*; it's something you already *have*. The mind has its own "self-clearing" function, capable of guiding you back to clarity, regardless of what state (or circumstances) you're in. While this is extremely evident in small children, all but a fortunate few have it conditioned out of them by the time they reach adulthood.

As you start to deepen your understanding of innate thinking, you're going to reconnect with your mind's natural self-clearing function. As a result, you'll find that you start having a) an effortlessly clear mind, b) more time for what's important, c) improved decision making, d) better performance where it counts and e) more of the results that matter to you. Some of the "side effects" you may notice include improving relationships, reducing stress levels, more passion and an increasing engagement with life.

4 *Why do we need clarity now, more than ever?* We're living at a pivotal point in history; millions of people are faced with uncertainty, complexity and increasing chaos. As individuals, as organizations and as an entire species, clarity is the key to solving the big issues

that face us, if we want to create a sustainable future for ourselves, and the generations that follow us.

In 2011, I made a commitment to the 80,000 members of my online community that I would send out an early draft of some of the material in this book. People read the chapters and posted their comments, questions and feedback on Facebook pages, instantly sharing them with the people in *their* networks (something which would have been unimaginable even ten years earlier). In the 18 months between sharing those chapters and writing this introduction, the acceleration of communication, technology and information has continued. Apple's iPhone 5 sold out 20 times faster than the previous model (five million units on the launch weekend alone). In January 2012, the social media phenomenon Pinterest.com became the fastest site in history to reach the ten million user mark (it took less than two years). Facebook has just announced that it has over a billion active users (that's a seventh of the population of the planet).

Communication, technology and information: they're accelerating, getting more pervasive and more compelling, with no sign they will ever slow down. The benefits are significant; we're supported by a digital infrastructure that was unimaginable 30 years ago. But as the Western world continues transitioning from a manufacturing economy to a knowledge economy, it's hobbled by educational institutions, social structures and habitual ways of thinking developed for a bygone era of smokestacks, whistles and assembly-lines.

Our mental clarity is under attack! Hyperlinks, smartphones and social media voraciously consume our precious attention. And, as that attention gets gobbled up, our minds become over-revved, weary and congested. Clogged with everything from breaking news and text alerts, to fears, anxieties and limiting beliefs, the overcrowded, speedy mind is the single biggest cause of stress, lack of confidence and bad decisions. Mental congestion results in time poverty, strained relationships, fumbled goals, poor performance and unrealized potential.

And mental congestion is expensive. The painful cost to individuals in terms of anxiety, distraction and conflict has a devastating knock-on effect; the price businesses are paying for lack of clarity is astronomical. Decreased productivity, lack of employee engagement and stress-related illness are some of the more obvious costs. But there's a much bigger (and less visible) price being paid in terms of missed opportunities, untapped passions and squandered creativity. While businesses recognize that there's an issue, they're unclear about what the problem actually is. So they block Facebook, or ban mobile phones, never realizing that these are *symptoms* of the problem, not its cause. Like weeds taking over a flowerbed, the over-revved, busy mind is voraciously consuming our most precious resources.

"Disruptive" is the watchword, as business-as-usual quickly becomes a thing of the past. 15-year-old Nick D'Aloisio writes an app in his bedroom (Summly). It goes viral and attracts the attention of Yahoo and News International, as well as over a million dollars in funding. Twitter overtakes the news media as the fastest way to get a message out to the masses. Lean start-ups use technology and soft innovation to steal market share from long-established businesses. Companies that have built their success over decades using old-school strategy and long-term planning get hamstrung by teams of people who are agile, creative, resilient and responsive.

All of which presents us with a serious challenge: As our world becomes increasingly uncertain, complex and chaotic, we seem to have less and less time, attention and wisdom to navigate it with.

> *At a point in history when we most need clarity,*
> *it appears to be in shorter and shorter supply...*

And so we try to compensate, as individuals and as organizations. From time management to mindfulness, from speed-reading to positive thinking, we try to get back in control. And, at first, it looks like it's helping; we feel like we're back in the driving seat. But then we lose motivation, or forget to use the technique; our attention gets drawn elsewhere or we fail to apply what we've learned.

It's not working. And it's not your fault.

Without even realizing it, we've been using an industrial-age *misunderstanding* of how the mind works to try to deal with the challenges of a digital world. As you continue reading this book, you're going to start undoing the conditioning that's been keeping you from clarity until now, and notice yourself experiencing a clear mind more and more frequently (with all the benefits it brings). At the times when your mind *is* clouded, you'll know what to do (and more importantly, what *not* to do). The conditioning is based in three main areas:

1 *Superstitious thinking: the outside-in misunderstanding.* This widespread piece of cultural conditioning mistakenly attributes clarity (and the lack of it) to a variety of circumstances. While this can easily be shown not to be the case, the conditioning is extremely persistent when it goes unchallenged. You're going to be introduced to a relaxing and enjoyable way of reading that will help you to "see through" this conditioning, and begin having insights and realizations that will make a difference to you immediately. As you deepen your understanding of innate thinking, you'll find stale habits of superstitious thinking dropping away, and clarity emerging to take their place.

2 *The move from a manufacturing economy to a knowledge economy.* Just as factory workers need to keep their machines clean and well oiled, knowledge workers, creatives, managers and leaders need to take similar care of their minds. Individuals and businesses are paying the price as time-scarcity, attention-poverty and information-saturation clog the "mental machinery" we rely on. But there's good news. People are born with a powerful immune system that protects us from disease and illness. The immune system reflects an innate tendency towards health and wellness that also shows up in the body's ability to repair wounds, breaks and other injuries. It is a little-known fact, however, that people also have a "psychological immune system," able to quickly restore even an extremely perturbed mind to clarity and well-being. As your understanding of innate

thinking continues to deepen, you'll find the clarity, intuition and resilience you need to prosper in times of uncertainty, complexity and change.

3 *Attempting to find clarity using outside-in methods.* The mind is a self-correcting system. The primary condition needed for a self-correcting system to find its way back to balance is simple: an absence of external interference. Outside-in methods such as positive thinking, affirmations and other techniques are examples of external interference. Other examples include smoking, drinking too much and internet addiction. While they can be used to clear the mind in the short term, they are not sustainable. In the long run, they often make matters worse if they give the busy-minded person even more to think about and do (I'm assuming that the last thing you need is more on your mind).

As you read this book, there's nothing you need to do, think about or implement...

- You won't need new regimes, systems or processes to remember.

- You won't be given lists of techniques, tactics or interventions to put into practice.

- You won't have to reframe, monitor or manage your thinking.

The book is designed to effortlessly activate your innate capacity for clarity. As you're going to discover, innate thinking will take care of the implementation for you.

DISTINCTION: Acting it vs. Catching it

If you've ever pretended to have a cold (perhaps while phoning in sick to work), you'll know that it's not that easy or convincing. It's tough to fake a sneeze, never mind the other unpleasant symptoms. This is an example of **acting it**. Most business and personal development books aim at giving you the things to think, change and do so you can "act" in a certain way to get the results you want.

On the other hand, when you genuinely *have* a cold, the symptoms emerge effortlessly. They're entirely convincing because they're *real*. This is an example of **catching it**. This book is designed so that you can "catch" an understanding that's more closely aligned with how your mind and life really work. As you catch the understanding, it will spontaneously result in the "symptoms" of increasing clarity, resilience and peace of mind, with all the other qualities and behaviours that naturally proceed from those states.

For this reason, the book has been designed differently from a traditional business or personal development book. It doesn't contain lists of things to do or key points to remember, and doesn't attempt to be coolly objective. Instead, it includes:

- Distinctions like the one above, clarifying important points.

- Simple "thought experiments" that you can conduct in less than a minute.

- Mini case studies from the experiences of my corporate and personal clients.

- Real-world stories as well as numerous metaphors and analogies.

- Scientific explanations expressed in down-to-earth terminology.

- Examples from history, current events and popular culture.

- Personal details and anecdotes from my own life.

- Reality checks where necessary.

- Diagrams and illustrations.

While you may find yourself reading this book again and again, you don't have to work at it. You're going to start seeing that you have a lot more going for you than you may have realized until now. One suggestion: this book is cumulative; Part Two and Part Three have plenty of interesting case studies and business examples, but they will not make much sense until you've read Part One. Your first time through, I strongly encourage you to read this book from the beginning.

It may sound like a bold claim, but the understanding you're going to be exposed to is, quite literally, effortless. The changes you can expect to see as you start to get a feel for innate thinking share three important qualities:

1 Your changes will be *natural*; a perfect fit to who you are.

2 Your changes will be *sustainable*; it's time to say goodbye to struggle and backsliding.

3 Your changes will be *generative*. This means that the positive impact of what you'll be learning will show up in many different aspects of your life, without you having to "make it happen."

As you read this book, you may be struck by the universal nature of what you're learning. People are often stunned that no one has ever told them this before. Paradoxically, they also remark that they've always known this on some level. As you start to experience the profound impact of increasing clarity in your own life, you may start to notice yourself feeling more optimistic and hopeful for your fellow human beings. Clarity is our best bet if we are to meet the challenges of our rapidly changing world, and leave a sustainable legacy for the generations to come.

But that's for later. The first step is for you to start discovering just how much *more* you've got going for you than you've previously imagined (even if you already know you've got a lot going for you). I want to assure you that you have the capacity for sustainable clarity, and all the benefits it brings. But first, a question:

Q: If you're caught in a trap, what's the one thing you have to do before you can escape?

A: You have to realize that you've been caught in a trap.

Until you realize you've been caught in a trap, you're very unlikely to get out of it. But once you know about the trap, and you can see how it works, then escape is pretty straightforward. Especially if other people have escaped from the same trap, and can show you how.

So please allow me to reveal the trap that's ensnared millions of people, including me…

---

keep exploring ❖ connect with others
share your discoveries ❖ deepen your understanding

At the end of each chapter, you'll find a section containing a reflection point. This is a statement or question that will help you integrate what you are learning even more deeply. For example:

Reflection point: *We each experience greater clarity from time to time. As you look back now, what are some of the more memorable occasions when you've found yourself experiencing an unexpected increase in clarity?*

When you reach a reflection point, pause for a moment. You don't have to figure out the question or "get it right". You don't even have to answer it. Just reading the question and reflecting on it for a moment is enough to continue your process of integration.

This section will also contain a website URL to enter into your browser and a QR code that you can scan using your smartphone. These will take you to web pages containing material relating to the chapter you've just read, ranging from videos and audio recordings to shareable articles, photos and infographics. In addition to the resources, you'll find features that allow you to post your comments and share what you're learning with others.

Experience shows that sharing your discoveries is a simple but powerful way for you to continue integrating what you're learning, as your understanding of innate thinking continues to deepen. I encourage you to explore, comment on and share these resources as you make your way through the book. You can start now…

www.ClarityBook.biz/introduction

PART ONE

The Essential Foundations

1

Misunderstanding: The Hidden Trap

"None are more hopelessly enslaved than those who falsely believe they are free."

Johann Wolfgang von Goethe,
Poet, playwright, novelist
and philosopher

"An addict is someone who's trying to use a visible solution to solve an invisible problem..."

I was no stranger to addiction when I heard this. I started drinking when I was 12 years old and didn't stop for good until I was 30. In the process of recovering from alcoholism, I explored a variety of approaches ranging from the spiritual to the material and all points in between.

I found value in much of what I learned, and my life improved in ways that I didn't even imagine were possible. But, in the process, I discovered an even deeper addiction, one that sits at the very heart of modern culture. This addiction is so subtle, it's almost *invisible*; a superstitious and life-eroding trap that has hooked countless millions of people; the trap I call "the *hidden hamster wheel.*"

The hidden hamster wheel

As you're going to discover, the hidden hamster wheel is a pervasive example of superstitious thinking, and one of the most common barriers to clarity.

It's based in a superstition that's taken to be "obviously true" by most of modern society. It's so subtle and pervasive that it shows up in everything from children's books to leadership programmes; from movies to marketing campaigns.

When a person deeply believes in a superstition, it informs everything they believe, everything they do, and how they do it. When a culture believes in a superstition, it gets reinforced from all sides.

The Power of Misunderstanding

In the 1800s, it was widely accepted that illnesses such as cholera and the plague were caused by "bad air" (also known as atmospheres or miasmas). At the time, huge numbers of people were moving to Soho in London, with an associated increase in sewage. The council of the day decided to dump the excess waste into the River Thames, unknowingly contaminating the water supply.

The impact was felt in 1854 when the Broad Street cholera outbreak claimed the lives of 618 Soho residents in just a few weeks. The physician, John Snow, was sceptical of the miasma theory, and managed to trace the epidemic to a water pump in Broad Street. His analysis of the outbreak pattern was compelling enough that the council removed the pump handle and the epidemic ended.

The miasma theory was a misunderstanding that was seen as fact. As a result, the decision to pump sewage into the water supply was taken from *within* that misunderstanding. While you and I know it's crazy to let human waste anywhere near your water supply, that's because we have a better understanding of how the world works; an understanding that just wasn't available to the people trapped within the miasma misunderstanding.

Misunderstanding can lead to needless misery, suffering and even death. But as soon as people get a clearer understanding of the nature of reality *as it already is*, there can be a massive and widespread improvement in quality of life.

John Snow, Joseph Lister, Ignatz Semmelweis and others had insights that allowed them to see through the misunderstandings of the time, leading to the creation of germ theory and modern medicine. As a result, millions of people are alive today who *wouldn't* be if we were still living in the miasma-theory superstition.

Thought Experiment

Imagine this: It's 1853, you live in Soho, London. It's crowded and smelly, so you're in the habit of carrying a small bunch of flowers to protect you from illness; a posy. Everyone you know does the same thing, and the posy industry is big business.

Then, one day, you meet a scientist who's convinced that diseases aren't caused by bad smells; that they're transmitted by tiny *invisible* creatures he calls "germs" and "bacteria." Would you believe it? Maybe, maybe not. Most people would probably say, *"Don't be silly – it's not as simple as that. Everybody knows that illness is caused by bad smells. It's obvious..."*

An essential question

If you were to be presented with the evidence that one of the most widely-held beliefs of modern society was in fact a misunderstanding about how life works, would you be able to listen with an open mind? The fact that you're reading this means that the answer is probably "Yes," so here goes...

The life-damaging misunderstanding that I call the *hidden hamster wheel* is the mistaken idea that our "core states" such as security, confidence, peace, love, happiness and success can be provided or threatened by our circumstances; by something "visible."

We have it because we've been conditioned to believe that there's somewhere to get to, and that "there" is better than "here." And "there" comes in a variety of tantalizing flavours that look something like this:

I'll be [*happy/secure/fulfilled/peaceful/better/successful/ok*] when I...

- Get the money/the car/the yacht/the house – the "there" of *stuff.*

- Find the right work/hobby/exercise/pastime – the "there" of *doing.*

- Have the right partner/friends/children – the "there" of *people and relationships.*

- Write the book/start the business/learn the language – the "there" of *accomplishment.*

- Can take a year off/travel the world/eat at the best restaurants – the "there" of *lifestyle.*

- Achieve time freedom/financial freedom/social freedom – the "there" of *freedom.*

- Lose the weight/stop smoking/start going to the gym – the "there" of *self-improvement.*

- Change my thinking/my limiting beliefs/do my affirmations – the "there" of *mindset.*

- Meditate properly/find the right practice/get enlightened – the "there" of *spirituality.*

- Accept myself/love myself/just let go – the "there" of *surrender.*

You may have experimented with none, some or all of the above. You may have made big changes and improved your life in a variety of ways. Or maybe not. At times, you may have felt like you're nearly there, like you're very close, like the pot of gold's just around the corner. And yet...

No matter how close you get, doesn't it always seem like there's a little more you need to do? A little further to go? Just a little bit more to fix, change or improve? Or a lot more?

I know, because I've done it – virtually everything on this list and more. I got value from many of my efforts but, sooner or later, after a week or a month or a year, I'd find myself feeling in some ways like I was back where I started, feeling like there was something missing, something wrong, something I couldn't quite put my finger on...

As it turns out, the story behind that sense of "something missing" doesn't just stop people from enjoying their lives to the full – it often stands in the way of having the life you really want. You see, as strange as it may sound, we've fallen into a trap. And it's a trap that's so subtle, most of us have never even noticed it. Subtle, powerful and all-pervasive.

The *"I'll be happy when..."* trap is an example most people can identify with. The core states and circumstances vary, but the basic structure of the superstition is the same:

> I'll be [*core state*] when I have [*circumstance*]

It's based on an even simpler structure:

> [*circumstance*] causes [*core state*]

And like pieces of Lego, this simple structure can be used to assemble all kinds of larger structures:

> I couldn't be [*core state*] if I lost [*circumstance*]
>
> I'm [*core state*] because of [*circumstance*]
>
> I can't be [*core state*] because I don't have [*circumstance*]
>
> I was [*core state*] until I lost [*circumstance*]
>
> I'm convinced that [*core state*] comes from [*circumstance*]

They can take a variety of shapes but, at heart, they're all based on the idea that our felt experience of life comes from our circumstances, from something relatively visible.

You may have seen studies showing that feelings of well-being and high self-esteem come from accomplishments, or from doing vocational work, or from meditating. But that's all an example of the superstition in action. When I use the word "circumstance," I'm using it in the widest possible way, to refer to pretty much anything you can imagine, including:

- Physical environment (e.g. home, holiday destination, workspace).

- What a person does (e.g. work, hobbies, exercise).

- Techniques (e.g. meditation, affirmations, reframing).

- Stuff (e.g. houses, boats, cars).

- Status (e.g. job title, position, medals).

- Material wealth (e.g. money, shares, income).

- People (e.g. partners, friends, children).

- Etc.

The idea that our core states are, at least to some degree, the result of our circumstances seems so "obvious" to people that calling it into question can seem ridiculous at first.

And while many people who have explored the domains of "brain-change" (through NLP, spirituality, personal development, meditation etc.) would say that they *know* that their core states don't come from their circumstances, their behaviour often suggests that they *don't* really know it.

In fact, people often replace one set of circumstances with a "higher level" version of the same thing...

- I'll be happy when I change my limiting beliefs.

- I'll feel fulfilled when I know that I'm on-purpose and doing work I love.

- I'll be on-track once I become an authentic leader.

- I'll feel secure when I'm generating passive income.

- I'll feel a sense of freedom when I have the lifestyle I want.

- I'll be able to enjoy myself when I retire.

- I'll be OK when I go on the next course/read the book/do the exercises – etc.

The circumstances may be different but the superstitious structure is still in place:

[*circumstance*] causes [*core state*]

Once again: we've been conditioned into the superstitious thinking that our clarity, security and well-being come from outside of us; that there's somewhere to get to, and that "there" is better than "here."

Reality Check

"Don't be silly!" I hear you say. *"Everybody knows that circumstances give us feelings. I'll give you some examples right now...*

- *"My sense of security comes from the fact that I've got a good job, and money in the bank.*

- *"I feel a sense of love and connection because I've found the right partner.*

- *"I feel stressed out because I've got a high-pressure business.*

- *"I feel peaceful when I go for a walk in the park.*

- *"I feel relaxed when I go on holiday.*

"Are you really trying to tell me that these examples are just a superstition? That my work doesn't actually stress me out? That my security doesn't come from money? That I don't feel love because of my partner? That I don't like going on holiday?"

Yes and no.

Your examples of your experience are real for you. I'm sure you can identify numerous circumstances where you experience certain feelings. I'm not saying you don't enjoy the things you enjoy, or that you shouldn't want the things that you want. What I'm saying is that the feelings aren't the result of the circumstances – they're coming from something else entirely. And, as you start to understand where they're coming from, and how the system works, some wonderful things can start to happen.

But I'm getting ahead of myself.

These days, I experience more clarity than I ever thought possible, with all the considerable benefits it brings. But I didn't get here in the way you might expect.

In brief: I grew up in an alcoholic household and started drinking heavily when I was 12 years old. By age 19, I was a scholarship engineering student and a full-blown alcoholic. The alcohol was like rocket fuel for my life – I got jobs, was promoted rapidly, and started experiencing many of the trappings of success – expense accounts, foreign travel, luxurious surroundings – but on the inside, I was slowly falling apart.

At the age of 30 I got married. A month later, her bags were packed; so I decided to stop drinking in order to save my relationship.

Oh yeah – I missed one. I'll be happy when I get a cigarette/a drink/a line of coke – the "there" of *addiction*.

That was in 1996, and I haven't had a drink since. Today I live a fulfilling life that's beyond anything I dreamed was possible for me, but how I got here is a story of struggle, frustration and heartbreak (much of which I could have avoided if I'd known what you're going to be discovering in this book).

Just to give you an idea, in the time-period from 1996 to 2008, I...

- Got married, had two daughters and moved to London.

- Managed several multi-million pound projects and became fascinated with the process of how individuals and organizations change.

- Was paralyzed by a combination of fear of failure and fear of success (I felt like I was a fraud, always worrying that I'd be "found out").

- Read hundreds of personal development books and went on dozens of courses.

- Quit my job and became a consultant, doing strategy workshops, team-building, executive coaching and training.

- Tried my hand at stand-up comedy and overcame my fear of public speaking (mainly by doing lots of public speaking).

- Lost weight, gained weight, lost weight, gained weight, lost weight, gained weight etc.

- Spent countless hours talking to a Freudian psychoanalyst and participated in various addiction recovery programmes.

- Learned NLP (neuro-linguistic programming), built a successful training company and grew a tribe of over 80,000 people.

- Was left by my wife, and struggled with worry, anxiety, depression and suicidal thoughts.

- Had numerous false horizons, thinking I'd finally "got it," only to find myself feeling like I was back where I started.

By the end of 2008, I was unhappy, stressed-out and at the end of my tether. I felt like I'd been giving it everything I had for over a decade. While some areas of my life were better than ever, in many ways I felt like I'd been running on the spot. I had many of the circumstances of success (passive income, time-freedom, foreign travel etc.), but I wasn't having a *feeling* of success. I was on the verge of giving up.

I understood *intellectually* that material success wouldn't give me a more profound and fulfilling experience of life, but I'd been *conditioned* into believing it would. The trick of the mind that tells us that our feelings come from somewhere other than our thinking is both persuasive and persistent.

Then I was introduced to the understanding you're going to be discovering in this book. As I write, it's four years on, and they've been the best years of my life. I'm experiencing a sense of clarity, peace, security and aliveness unlike anything I've had before. And as my level of understanding has continued to increase, my relationships, results and external circumstances have been improving too.

The good news is that it can be replicated. My clients are getting similar results, including:

- less stress, more clarity and peace of mind;

- being more creative and innovative, finding solutions to problems more easily;

- better working relationships, and more harmony in their personal lives;

- being more productive, getting more done and having more free time;

- better business results, and better performance where it counts;

- fears, anxieties and limitations falling away effortlessly;

- natural motivation, making real progress with the things that matter;

- better health, with more vibrancy and aliveness.

It's working for them, so it can work for you; because seeing through a superstition can give you an "out of proportion" increase in the results you get. Why? Because a superstition is really just a misunderstanding, based on a piece of flawed logic. A simple misunderstanding that often leads to unwanted...

Stress	Worry	Addiction	Poverty
Pressure	Anxiety	Mental illness	Bullying
Poor productivity	Irritation	Depression	Criminality
Dissatisfaction	Frustration	Burnout	Violence
Conflict	Resentment	Divorce	etc.

So how do you escape from this addictive, life-damaging trap? How do you start seeing through the misunderstanding, and begin to experience an enormous increase in clarity and quality of life?

keep exploring ⟡ connect with others
share your discoveries ⟡ deepen your understanding

Reflection point: We all fall into the "I'll be happy when..." trap from time to time. As you reflect on your life so far, what are some of the ways you now realize you've been accidentally hoodwinked by this illusion?

Once you've taken a minute or two to reflect, you can share whatever you've discovered. Just scan the QR code with your smartphone or type the URL below into your browser. In addition to posting your comments and sharing what you're learning with others, you'll also find powerful *Clarity* resources relating to Chapter 1 – Misunderstanding: The Hidden Trap. Experience shows that this is a simple but powerful way for you to continue integrating what you're discovering, as your understanding of innate thinking continues to deepen...

www.ClarityBook.biz/chapter1

2

The Power of Insight

"We cannot teach people anything; we can only help them discover it within themselves."

Galileo Galilei,
Astronomer, physicist
and mathematician

"Don't take this the wrong way, but I get the impression that you haven't been listening very well until now..."

This sentence caught me by surprise. My new coach didn't know it, but I was renowned for my listening skills. I had trained for many years to notice fine distinctions in voice tone and body language, and could unpack the deep structures of what a person was saying, moment to moment. The idea that I wasn't a good listener seemed preposterous to me. But I was curious, so I asked what he meant.

My coach explained, very gently, that when I was listening, it seemed like I had a lot on my mind. I was "doing" listening; it was something I was working at. He said that listening in this way was OK for getting an intellectual understanding of something, but it wasn't going to help me have the clarity and insights that could really make a difference in my life.

As I reflected on it, I realized that this is how we've *all* been taught to listen. It's how we've been taught to read. It's how we've been "taught" to learn.

But it used to be different.

You were born a listener and learner. It's thanks to these natural abilities that you can walk and talk today. You knew how to listen long before anyone ever "taught" you how to think; before you knew how to analyze and judge; before you were taught that analysis and judgement had any value.

If you're anything like me, you were taught to read, listen and learn for an *intellectual understanding*, and that's fine as far as it goes. But it's time to remember a different way to read, listen and learn: reading for insight...

> ## DISTINCTION: Reading for information vs. Reading for insight
>
> When most people read, they're trying to fit what they're reading into what they already know, seeing how the new information can slot into their existing cognitive structure. This is **reading for information**; looking to verify and build upon what you know. But there's another way of reading. You can read in a way that creates a space for an "intuitive knowing" that already exists within your consciousness to emerge more fully into your awareness. This is **reading for insight**.

Reading for information

When we read for information, we think about what we're reading as we're reading it, making decisions about...

- whether or not we agree with it
- where it fits into our existing cognitive structures
- if it doesn't fit, why not?
- whether to accept or reject it
- if/how we're going to apply it
- etc.

Just check – you may be doing this as you're reading this passage, saying *"I must remember this," "That makes sense," "That's nonsense"* or somewhere in between. That's OK. Reading for information can be useful when you're evaluating data, and making decisions about its validity. But the huge increase in the sheer *volume* of information available means that reading in this way is often contributing to mental congestion. It moves us further away from clarity. A person who's reading for information has "something on their mind," so the mind isn't free to do what it does best – generate fresh, clear thinking.

When it comes to clarity,
reading for information
is like drinking salt water;
it just makes you more thirsty...

Reading for insight

Reading for insight is reading with "nothing on your mind." When you read for an insight, you put your existing conceptual models to one side and allow yourself to be impacted by what you're reading.

The magic eye

Back in the 1990s, evolving technology led to the creation of "magic-eye" images. At first glance, a magic-eye image looks like a repeating, two-dimensional pattern, but if you look "through" the image, with a soft-eyed, relaxed gaze, something amazing happens. A three-dimensional figure suddenly leaps into your awareness, a figure that was totally invisible when you first looked at the image.

People often sat staring at the 2D images, "trying hard" to see the 3D image hidden within it, but nothing happened until they relaxed and allowed the image to emerge.

Reading for an insight is sort of like looking at a magic-eye picture. You don't really need to "think about" what you're reading – you just relax and allow yourself to be impacted by the words. The insight that can clear your mind and give you fluid, fresh thinking isn't in the words anyway; it's a capacity that's right there inside of you, "pre-loaded" into your consciousness.

Another example is music. When you listen to music you enjoy, you're not trying to decide whether you agree with it or not. You're listening to be impacted; to enjoy it and have an experience. When you're reading or listening for insight, you "get a feel" for what the person's saying, seeing beyond the written (or spoken) word to what the author's really trying to convey. You allow an intuitive knowing to emerge from within your consciousness (this is what's happening when you get a sudden "a-ha.")

The power of insight

To get a feel for the difference between intellectual understanding and insightful understanding, imagine a dog that's constantly chasing his tail. Now let's imagine that the dog hires you and me as consultants to help him with overall productivity. We ask the dog what he needs, and he says something like this:

"Here's what I need: First, I need more speed, because the thing I'm chasing is very fast. It always seems to be able to outrun me. Second, I need more agility, because this thing is also very nimble. Even when I creep up on it, it manages to slip away before I can catch it. Third, I need better strategy, because no matter what I do, it always seems one step ahead of me. It's almost as if it knows what I'm thinking! Finally, I need more time. I'm already working 12-hour days on this, and it just doesn't seem to be enough. So that's what I need; more speed, more agility, better strategy and more time."

You and I both know that all the dog *really* needs is to realize that it's *his own tail* he's been chasing. But if we tell him that, there are two ways the dog might respond. If he insightfully understands what we tell him, and really "gets it," then he will visibly relax, sigh and maybe even chuckle. He might say:

"That really makes sense. It's a load off my mind, and it sure explains a lot of things which had been puzzling me until now. It's also taken a lot off my to-do list, and I've suddenly got a lot more space in my diary. I've got to admit, I'm feeling a bit sheepish, but it sure is a relief. Thanks for all the extra time!"

On the other hand, if the dog has an *intellectual* understanding, but doesn't have an insight, he might say something like this:

> "Right. So you're telling me that it's my tail. Got it. So I need to remember not to chase it, right? OK. So how do I not chase my tail? Can you just take me through the process?"
>
> If the dog says this, we know that he hasn't really understood.

The *biggest* value you're going to get from this book isn't going to come from the information on the pages – the biggest value is going to come from inside you, so allow space for that to happen. Any intellectual understanding you already have will still be available when you get to the end of the book, so I invite you to put that to one side and allow yourself to be even more deeply impacted.

The reality is that every person has this source of insight within them. You have everything you need to bring you to clarity. The power behind the changes you make is going to come from within you. As you read this book for an insight, you may occasionally find yourself feeling particularly clear, calm and peaceful. That sense of clarity can be one of the signs that you're being impacted, so enjoy it when it comes and relax when it doesn't..

And what's so great about insight?
Insightful understanding often arrives suddenly, but can continue serving and informing you for years to come. It's a natural function of the mind, and has the power to make the changes that matter in your life. Insight is the key to re-connecting you with your mind's self-clearing capacity.

When you read (or listen) for *information*, the intellectual understanding you get is like a written instruction manual; it's good as far as it goes, but it takes effort to put it into practice. That's why people often say *"I understand that intellectually, but…"*

Insightful understanding is more like an app for a mobile phone – once it's downloaded, it starts working immediately. Insightful understanding is powered up and ready to go!

Remember in the Introduction, when I said there's nothing in this book that you need to do, think about or implement?

- When you have an insight, it comes with its own source of motivation. You don't need to "get yourself to do it" – you're going to find your behaviour changing naturally in ways that serve you.

- When you have an insight, it's tailored exactly for you. You don't have to figure it out or try and adjust it to your needs – it already fits you perfectly.

- Insightful understanding is context sensitive, and can adjust to your changing circumstances, even taking account of things you're not consciously aware of.

- Intellectual understandings can get stale over time, but insightful understandings stay fresh, and can keep "updating your system" for years to come.

That's why people so often know what they "should" be doing, but don't do it. Until you have an insight, it's just a nice idea. The great news is that insights start making a difference to you whether they make sense intellectually or not!

A sudden insight

In the 1990s I was employed as a programme director, running large organizational change programmes for global businesses. After running a number of successful programmes, I wanted to leave my job and become a contractor. My friends assured me I could do it and, while I understood that *intellectually*, I "knew" that I didn't have what it took. Then, in 1998, I attended my first personal development training – a two-day programme about the workings of the mind. During the two days, I had an insight: I suddenly *knew* that I could leave my job and become a contractor, with all the freedom, possibilities and rewards that entailed. I quit my job two weeks later, started working for myself and creating the time and money to follow my passions. I can trace the life I have today back to that insight, and can still feel the sense of freedom and possibility it brought me.

While the example above was massively transformational for me, insightful understanding is an everyday phenomenon. In fact, as you start to become more and more aware of it, you'll begin to find yourself relying on insights and intuition to guide you on a day-to-day basis.

Everyone has had the experience of making a bad decision, then saying *"I knew I should have done it the other way, but I didn't listen to myself."* Many people also have examples of "just know-ing" the right thing to do, even though it doesn't seem logical at the time. The intuitive knowing that they're referring to is an example of insightful understanding. People have many ways of referring to it:

- The gut feeling that lets you know to take a certain decision.

- The common sense that saves the day in a difficult situation.

- The intuition that leads you to an unexpected success.

- The sudden realization that makes a big difference in your life.

- The "knowing" that has you ask just the right question.

- The insight that solves a problem that looked like it was impossible.

- The creative leap that takes things in a whole new direction.

- The "moment of clarity" that turns an addict's life around.

- The inspiration that gives you fresh, new energy and motivation.

- The inner wisdom that guides you in situations where your old ideas no longer apply.

Most people don't realize how powerful insight is when it comes to finding clarity, making changes and delivering the goods. And while this book is full of ideas that you may find interesting and informative, its *real* power is in creating a context; a context where the intuitive knowing that's *already there within you* can emerge more fully into your awareness and make a real difference in your life.

In fact, the essential difference between this and most other books is this:

The purpose of this book is to act as a catalyst so that your own insights and realizations can bring you to clarity, guiding you and helping you make changes as you move forward.

Insightful understanding comes from innate thinking; your natural ability to have fresh, clear perceptions at any moment. It's a power that already exists within your consciousness and can show up in ways that make a difference in your life instantly.

Reality Check

Sometimes people object, saying that clarity is not "fresh, clear thinking," but is in fact an *absence* of thoughts. That is both true and not true. As you're going to discover, clarity is the result of a more fluid and unobtrusive kind of thinking. If habitual, stuck patterns of thought are like white-water rapids, clarity of thought is like the deep, clear waters of a flowing river. That's why so many people who are in the flow say they have nothing on their mind.

So I invite you to "read for an insight" as we start exploring a phenomenon that's very strange, entirely counterintuitive and still one of the most *shocking* things I've ever encountered...

keep exploring ❖ connect with others
share your discoveries ❖ deepen your understanding

Reflection point: Insight is a natural part of being alive. Sometimes, small, everyday insights end up being as profound as the big "a-has." As you think about it now, what are some of your more useful and impactful insights and a-ha moments so far?

One of the great things about insights is that when you see something, you can shine a light on it for other people, too. And when you share it, you remind yourself of the truth of the matter. To share some of your insights, just scan the QR code with your smartphone or type the URL below into your browser. You'll be able to access powerful *Clarity* resources relating to Chapter 2 – The Power of Insight. You'll also find features that allow you to post your comments and share what you're learning with others. When you externalize your thoughts by writing them down, it actually creates new neural pathways in your brain, supporting new perspectives and deeper understanding...

www.ClarityBook.biz/chapter2

3

How Perception is Created

"Thought creates the world then says 'I didn't do it'"

David Bohm, Quantum physicist

"Now in a dream, our mind continuously does this... We create and perceive our world simultaneously... And our mind does this so well that we don't even know it's happening..."

These words are spoken by Leonardo DiCaprio, playing the lead character, Cobb, in the film *Inception* (2010, Warner Bros. Pictures). He's drawing a circle made of two arrows and explaining how dreams work, but his explanation also shines a light on the nature of our waking perception. When we're awake, our experience is generated in exactly the same way (albeit with access to a "live data feed"). To paraphrase Cobb:

> *"In your waking experience of reality, your mind continuously creates and perceives a world simultaneously... So well that you don't feel your mind doing the creating."*

When you stop and deeply consider the implications of this, it can be truly shocking. It means that 100% of your experience of the world "outside" of you is actually taking place "inside" you. This includes the bits that you see "out there."

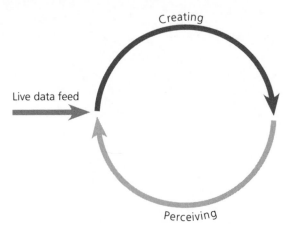

Figure 3.1 Simultaneously Creating and Perceiving

Your experience of the world "out there" is being generated from inside you, incorporating data received by the senses to a greater or lesser degree (depending on your focus of attention).

For example, a person can be asleep and dreaming that they're in the front row at a rock concert, only to wake up and discover that the music in their dream was coming from the radio next to their bed. Conversely, a person can be sitting in a business meeting, but have their focus of attention entirely absorbed by a daydream about a future holiday. Whether the data is arriving from your senses, your memories, or your imagination, the process that's *generating* your perceptual experience is the same.

*Our experience of reality is, quite literally, created
from "the stuff that dreams are made of."*

Perceptual Adaptation

The psychologist, George Stratton, performed a series of intriguing experiments in the 1890s using a pair of "inversion glasses." These curious glasses presented the wearer's eyes with an inverted image of reality – they turned everything upside down! Stratton himself wore the glasses for eight days straight. For the first four days, he was presented with an upside-down world, but when he woke up on the fifth day of wearing them, something extraordinary had happened; his perception had corrected itself, and he now perceived the world the right way up.

Another surprise followed when he removed the glasses; he found that reality now looked upside down when he *wasn't* wearing them. It was a few days before his sight returned to normal. This phenomenon (referred to as "perceptual adaptation") highlights the creative role the mind plays in generating our moment-to-moment experience of reality.

Stop for a moment. Have a look around you. Listen to any sounds you're aware of. Run your fingers over some objects in your environment...

It might seem as though you are looking at the world "out there" through your eyes in much the same way as you look through the viewfinder of a camera, but that's not how it works. The truth of our perception is entirely different and far, far stranger. You see...

*Your perception of reality is less like looking out at
the world through the lens of a camera, and more
like wearing a pair of virtual reality goggles...*

Have another look around you, and allow yourself to notice one
or two objects in your immediate environment. I know it looks as
though the objects are "out there" (and for practical purposes they
are) but 100% of your *experience* of the objects is being generated
from within your consciousness.

*The fabric of your experiential reality is
being generated by your mind...*

Reality Check

I'm not saying "you create your own reality"; I'm saying that you create
your own unique *experience* of reality, moment to moment, from within
your consciousness. We live in a material world that is governed by
inviolable laws that are not materially influenced by your perception
(e.g. gravity, thermodynamics etc.). If you're walking down the street
and fail to notice an uncovered manhole in your path, you're not going
to be able to glide over the manhole just because you don't realize it's
there. Gravity is a principle; a fundamental law governing our world. As
such, it's not bothered about what you or I think!

Energy streams in through all our senses simultaneously, creating
an intense, multi-sensory "snapshot" of each moment. The energy
flows in as raw data, in much the same way data flows into a computer through a USB port. The mind then creates a model of "what
must be out there for me to be receiving this data." This model is
what's "represented" to us in consciousness.

We've all had the experience of seeing a friend in the street, wav-
ing to them, then realizing it's not actually the person we thought
it was. Yet, a moment earlier, we could have sworn it was them.
When we first "saw" them, what we *actually* saw was a mind-
made perceptual "guess." It was only when we looked more closely

that a more accurate (but still mind-made) perception was created, based on fresh data.

Our perception is constantly making these sorts of "guesses," but we usually only become aware of the guessing process in situations like the example above, or when we look at an optical illusion.

Figure 3.2 The Kanizsa Triangle

As you look at the Kanizsa Triangle, raw data from the image is intercepted by your eyes and transmitted to your brain. Brain software enhances the data, filling in the gaps and voila! The perceptual reality generated by your mind includes an illusory white triangle. The brain has a huge variety of these "reality enhancement programmes," developed as survival advantages over countless millenia of evolution (e.g. the ability to discern sharp edges, recognize faces, and so on).

In his fascinating 2005 TED talk, "Why the universe seems so strange," biologist Richard Dawkins points out that we don't experience the "unvarnished world"; we experience a *model* of the world that's optimized for the type of creature we are, and the kind of world we inhabit. Birds need different kinds of models from monkeys; birds need to be able to deal with aerial navigation, while monkeys need software that allows them to climb trees and swing from branch to branch. Fish need different models from moles or ants, because they inhabit totally different environments, and are different types of creature. None of these creatures access the world directly; rather, they live in a mind-made *experiential* reality based on a model or representation that's suited to the type of creature they are, and the type of world they inhabit. It's the same with people.

*The fabric of your experiential reality is
being generated by your mind...*

The Pixels of Perception

I'm writing this book using an Apple MacBook. As I write, I can see the words I'm typing appearing on the screen. At any point, I can watch a YouTube video, flick through my photo library, search for a quote using Google, post something on Facebook or scroll through another document. But one thing remains constant...

Everything you can see on the screen is created using pixels.

Pixels are the tiny building blocks that are used to create the videos, the photographs, the letters in the documents, the images on the web pages... everything! It's all pixels.

Similarly, your experience of reality is made of the perceptual equivalent of pixels; an "energy" that I'm going to refer to as THOUGHT.

Thought Experiment

Again, look around at the environment you're in. As you notice the different elements in that environment, consider the fact that what you're seeing is actually a representation being generated by (and within) your amazing mind. Your experience of everything you can see is made of the pixels of perception; THOUGHT.

Now close your eyes and remember what you were able to see in your environment. Your memory of those things is also made of THOUGHT.

Now imagine an event you're planning to enjoy in the future. This future-memory is made of THOUGHT.

When you're asleep and dreaming, your dreams are made of THOUGHT. Every experience you have in your entire life is generated using the power of THOUGHT.

You create your own experience of reality, moment to moment, from within your consciousness, using the power of THOUGHT...

The CCTV mind

Imagine a security guard, watching a CCTV screen showing people walking past the entrance of the building she's responsible for. Light waves bounce off the passers-by, some of which are intercepted by the CCTV camera. At lightning speed, the camera translates the images into digital data, before transmitting the data to a computer system which generates an image on the CCTV screen. While there are definitely people walking past the building, 100% of what shows up on the CCTV screen has been generated by the computer.

Our security guard's heart leaps as she recognizes a face amongst the moving shapes on the screen! She's just recognized her lover arriving to take her for a romantic dinner. While the security guard may later claim that she "saw" her lover approaching, what she actually saw was a representation of her lover; a computer-generated illusion on a television screen.

This is a simple analogy for how we create our experience of reality, moment to moment. As I'm writing this, I can look out the window of the coffee shop I'm sitting in and see people walking past. While there are definitely people "out there," 100% of my *experience* of those people is a mind-made illusion.

The Gherkin and the bell curve

The iconic London skyscraper known as "The Gherkin" gets a variety of responses from people. Some experience it as a shining example of modern architecture; others experience it as a vile monstrosity. If you were to plot 1000 people's subjective experience of The Gherkin, a bell curve would emerge, with a range of responses. For each individual, 100% of their *experience* of The Gherkin would be coming from their thinking.

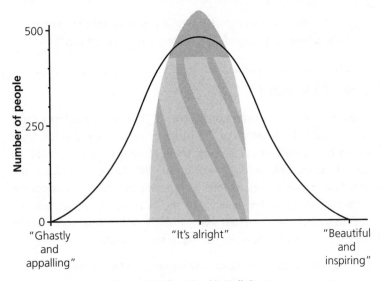

Figure 3.3 The Gherkin Bell Curve

Of course, the energy of THOUGHT isn't just limited to our visual experience. While we've used the visual metaphor of pixels for explanatory purposes, our experiences of sound, smell, taste, and touch are also "constructed" from THOUGHT. So are our feelings and emotions.

THOUGHT *is the reality principle...*

It's the power you have to create a representation of absolutely anything and experience it as real. We each live in a psychological reality. Our perceptual experience is 100% mind-made, using THOUGHT; the reality principle.

Reality Check

If you are scientifically-inclined you may be saying to yourself, *"Hang on a second, our perception isn't made of pixels or THOUGHT! It's made of synapses, neurons, neurochemicals and electrical currents!"*

Brain science is an incredibly valuable area of research, giving us a close-up view of the "mechanics" of brain functioning. There's no doubt that our brain structures make it possible to perceive in ways that just aren't available to creatures who don't have these structures (for example, the fusiform gyrus, which we use for facial recognition). These brain structures allow us to use THOUGHT in ways that wouldn't be possible without them, but our subjective experience is still created by what I'm calling THOUGHT. In fact, the word THOUGHT itself is just a metaphor for this incredible ability.

Here's another way of thinking about it: The London Underground system (aka "the Tube") is an incredibly complex network of tunnels, wires and tracks. While the electrical schematics of the underground system have to be incredibly accurate, they're not very useful for finding your way from Oxford Circus to King's Cross. For that, you're better off using the Tube map. The Tube map is a masterpiece of simplicity and functionality; incredibly useful for getting from A to B.

If brain chemistry is like the electrician's schematic (accurate, but abstract and incredibly complex), then the *Innate Thinking®* model is more like the Tube map – simple, subjective and highly practical once you get the hang of it.

People are literally able to think *anything* and experience it as real. The power of THOUGHT is so flexible that people can use it to create any perceptual reality:

- Two people watching the same movie can have two completely different experiences of it, thanks to THOUGHT.

- A person with a phobia uses THOUGHT to create the experience of an imminent plane crash, a spider bite or a dog attack.

- A person doing a job can feel inspired and energized, while the person sitting next to them feels stressed and unhappy doing *exactly the same work*. Both of them create their unique experience using THOUGHT.

- A person can become convinced that their business partner is cheating them, regardless of the reality of the situation. They create their perception using THOUGHT, then experience it as real.

- Someone can have a richly enjoyable experience, anticipating a holiday that they're planning to go on. THOUGHT is making that enjoyable experience possible, even if the holiday ends up being cancelled!

I'm not saying that we're doing this deliberately or consciously. I'm merely pointing to the capacity people have to create literally *any* perception using the incredible power of THOUGHT, and then experience that perception as real. This is how our experience is created, and we're using this capacity every moment of our lives.

The reason this is so relevant when it comes to escaping from the hidden hamster wheel and experiencing increasing levels of clarity is this:

100% of our experience of reality is mind-made. If a person thinks they need X, Y or Z in order to feel A, B or C, then they will experience that as a reality. That's how powerful THOUGHT is.

Do you remember the structure of the superstition/misunderstanding from Chapter One?

[*circumstance*] causes [*core state*]

THOUGHT has the power to bring each of the different permutations of this superstitious formula to life, and have a person experience it as a material reality. THOUGHT is like the special-effects department of a movie studio. Its job is to create a perceptual reality that looks real, regardless of the "facts" of the situation. But we can all think of times when we "knew" something to be true, then later discovered it was an illusion, because...

You can't take your THOUGHT-generated experiential reality at face value – it *always* looks real. That's its job. The sign of high-quality special effects is that you can't tell they're special effects; they look like the real thing.

And THOUGHT is the best special-effects department in the world. We're living in the experience of our thinking before we know thinking has anything to do with it!

So how does knowing this help us? And what does it have to do with clarity?

It turns out that the biggest obstacle to clarity is the result of a kind of "mental magic trick." Like so many magic tricks, its workings have been a secret until now. But it's time to reveal how the trick works. And like any magic trick... once you know how it's done, it's never the same again...

**keep exploring ⠿ connect with others
share your discoveries ⠿ deepen your understanding**

Reflection point: Take a few moments to look around you. Tune in to whatever sounds you hear, and become aware of any tactile sensations you can feel. What happens when you consider the fact that 100% of the experience of your senses is being generated by THOUGHT, moment to moment? That the fabric of your experiential reality "out there" is in fact being generated by your mind?

If you're anything like me, there's no verbal answer to those questions. You may, however, have a sense of confusion, puzzlement or even wonder at the extraordinary nature of perception. This is a *good* thing! Whatever your response is, I'd love you to share it. Just scan the QR code with your smartphone or type the URL below into your browser. Feel free to take a few minutes for yourself and explore the *Clarity* resources relating to this chapter before or after you post your comments...

www.ClarityBook.biz/chapter3

4

The Power of Principles

"Misdirection is the art of initiating a train of thought in the mind of the spectator."

Alan Alan, Escapologist
and illusionist

"It seems as though you've been thinking your happiness, security and general OK-ness is dependent on you achieving your goals..."

"Yes... Obviously!" I replied. I'd just finished explaining to one of my mentors why it was so vitally important that I achieve a particular objective.

"That means you don't understand where your security and well-being come from," he told me. *"Your happiness, security and OK-ness doesn't come from outside you, so it's not vulnerable to anything outside you."*

I'd fallen for a trick that's been bedevilling people for thousands of years. I'd been fooled into thinking my happiness and well-being was dependent on my circumstances.

DISTINCTION: Outside-in vs. Inside-out

Our experience of life is created from the **inside-out**, but it often *looks* as though it's created from the **outside-in**. This is because our experience of life is less like looking through the viewfinder of a camera, and more like wearing a pair of virtual reality goggles. Data streams in through our senses, and we generate an experience from the **inside-out**:

- **Inside-out**: *We're always living in the feeling of our thinking. 100% of our felt experience is always coming from Thought in the moment, from the **inside-out**. None of our experience is coming from anywhere other than Thought.*

- **Outside-in**: *Due to a trick of the mind, it often appears as though we're feeling something other than our moment-to-moment thinking; like our experience is being created from the **outside-in**. This illusion can be very compelling, but it never works that way (that's why it's called an illusion).*

History is full of these illusions and false appearances:

- **Flat earth vs. Spherical earth:** People used to think the earth was flat, *because that's how it looked to them.* But it was *never* flat; it was *always* spherical, with some bulging (officially its shape is described as an "oblate spheroid"). It's spherical 100% of the time, even when it looks like it isn't.

- **Geo-centric vs. Solar-centric:** People used to think that the sun went round the earth, because that's how it looked to them. But the sun *never* went round the earth; the earth *always* went round the sun. The earth goes round the sun 100% of the time, even when it looks like it doesn't.

Our experience is being generated from the **inside-out,** 100% of the time, even when it looks like it isn't. There are two basic mistakes of attribution that people tend to make because of the outside-in misunderstanding:

Mistake #1 – We tend to mistakenly attribute our fulfilling, enjoyable experiences to something other than thinking – to our circumstances, future hopes, past events, other people etc. But our fulfilling, enjoyable, desirable feelings are THOUGHT-generated; they only ever come from within us. We're always feeling the products of THOUGHT in the moment.

Examples:

- I'll be successful once I get the promotion.
- I feel good because I'm with you.
- I'm secure because I've got money in the bank.
- I'll have a sense of freedom once I quit my job.
- My dog makes me happy.
- I'm confident and outgoing because of my upbringing.

Our feelings, states and emotions can't possibly come from anywhere other than THOUGHT, because our experience is mind-made. We live in an "inside-out" world, and the experiences we enjoy only ever come from within us. Period.

Mistake #2 – We tend to mistakenly attribute our uneasy, unpleasant feelings to something other than thinking. Our uneasy, unpleasant, agitated feelings are THOUGHT-generated; they only ever come from within us. Like mistake #1, we're always feeling the products of THOUGHT in the moment.

Examples:

- I feel anxious about the job interview.

- I'm angry because of what my boss said.

- I'd be devastated if you left me.

- I'm afraid of failure.

- Your dog makes me nervous.

- I'm shy because of my upbringing.

As you can see, these two mistakes are the same misunderstanding. I'm not saying that job interviews, dogs, bosses, money and cars don't exist; I'm just saying that none of our feelings come from them. 100% of our experience of interviews, dogs, bosses, money and cars comes from within us – we're always living in the experience of our thinking, moment to moment.

Superstitious thinking: the outside-in misunderstanding

Misdirection is the master skill of the con-artist, the comedian and the magician.

Illusions and magic tricks work because of misdirection; the magician initiates a train of thought in the mind of the spectator, based on a false

THE POWER OF PRINCIPLES

assumption. Once the spectator has accepted the false assumption, they're likely to stay on that train of thought until "the reveal." The magician reaches into the empty hat and pulls out a rabbit! The cabinet is opened to reveal that the woman has vanished! The card in the magician's pocket turns out to be the one you picked! The sensations of surprise, confusion and delight are created at the moment the false train of thought is derailed. It's the same with comedy; we laugh at the moment our train of thought is revealed to have been based on a false assumption.

The false assumption that we're feeling something *other than* thinking in the moment is a misunderstanding.

It often looks as though our felt experience of life is coming from something other than the products of THOUGHT, but it doesn't work that way. Why? Because THOUGHT is always creating a perceptual reality. Our thinking always looks real to us.

> *Superstitious thinking, arising from the*
> *outside-in misunderstanding, is the only*
> *thing that ever keeps us from clarity.*

It has no basis in reality. It looks compelling and real, but it's spurious, groundless and bogus.

Imagine a snow-globe that's been vigorously shaken. The snow fills the entire globe, obscuring everything else. But the moment you set the snow-globe down, the snow starts to settle, and the liquid clears. Superstitious thinking is like the snow in the snow-globe; plentiful and impenetrable, but with no meaningful substance.

> *Clarity is like the liquid in a snow-globe. It's always there,*
> *behind the scenes, ready to start emerging the moment*
> *you insightfully see the inside-out nature of reality;*
> *the realization that you're feeling your thinking in the moment...*

It tends to look like we're each living in our *circumstances* (a world of jobs, friends, cars, family, houses, money, colleagues, accomplishments etc.) but we're each living in our mind-made *experience*.

And that THOUGHT-generated experiential reality is "brought to life" by the principles behind innate thinking.

Behind the scenes

In 1974, a Scottish welder named Sydney Banks living in Western Canada had a sudden, transformational insight into the nature of experience. In a matter of moments he went from being a middle-aged man riddled with anxieties and insecurities to being calm, clear and peaceful, with a profound understanding of how our experience of reality is created.

The *Oxford English Dictionary* describes a principle as "the fundamental source or basis for something." As time passed, Banks started to talk in these terms, explaining that our experience of life is generated from principles. You can think of these principles as the source of (and basis for) 100% of our experience. These are the fundamental principles behind innate thinking:

THOUGHT: *The reality principle*
People think. The principle of THOUGHT refers to our innate capacity to generate a perceptual reality; an outer and inner world that we can see, hear, feel, taste and smell. This principle is also the source of the countless thoughts and perceptions that arise in the course of a day.

CONSCIOUSNESS: *The experience principle*
People are aware. The principle of CONSCIOUSNESS refers to our capacity to have an *experience* of our thinking; it brings our THOUGHT-generated experiential reality to life. We're always living in the feeling of our thinking, and it's CONSCIOUSNESS that enables us to experience it.

MIND: *The power principle*
People are alive. The principle of MIND is the "intelligent energy" that shows up in all aspects of the natural world. MIND is the "power-source" behind life. Various cultures and fields have different names for this power: Life-force, universal energy, chi, nature, the great spirit, God, the no-thing, evolution, random chance etc. You can think of it in whatever way makes sense to you.

We spend our lives moving through a dizzying variety of experiential realities, many of which bear little or no relation to any *objective* reality (if you doubt this, just cast your mind back to your last sexual fantasy).

Let's use a simple metaphor; a desktop computer system. The desktop system consists of three main elements; a power supply, a screen, and the computer itself. We'll use each of these elements as a metaphor for one of the principles mentioned above:

- The power supply (MIND)
- The screen (CONSCIOUSNESS)
- The computer itself (THOUGHT)

MIND is like the computer's power supply; you can have the best computer in the world, but if it's not plugged in, it doesn't work. Just as computers have a power supply, you can think of people (and all living organisms) as having a "power supply" that animates us. Speaking metaphorically, we're plugged in rather than battery-operated.

CONSCIOUSNESS is like the computer's screen; you can press "play" on a favourite YouTube video, but if you switch the screen off, you can't see it. CONSCIOUSNESS is the "screen" that brings our thinking to life, and gives us an experience of our THOUGHT-generated realities.

THOUGHT is like the computer itself; there's nothing on the screen until you connect it to the computer. And just as the computer is the source of 100% of what shows up on the screen, THOUGHT is the source of 100% of the *form* of our experience.

So what's the point of learning about principles?

Principles are a source of massive leverage. When you understand the principles behind something, it increases your power exponentially. For example...

The principles of flight

People struggled for centuries to create flying machines. While people saw birds and insects flying, they didn't understand the principles that made flight possible. Then, the Wright brothers discovered the *principles* of aeronautics. In December 1903 they achieved the first manned, machine-powered flight. In the century since, the world of aeronautics has achieved extraordinary feats (the helicopter, the jump-jet, the space-shuttle and Concorde to name but a few). Discovering the principles of aeronautics gave people massive leverage to create things that couldn't even be dreamt of previously.

Reality Check

You may be saying, "Hang on a second! Gravity is a principle, but you can measure gravity. How can you measure THOUGHT, CONSCIOUSNESS and MIND?"

We *can't* actually see or measure gravity per se, because it's formless; but we can measure its effects. We know that if you drop a pencil, gravity will cause it to fall to the floor. By observing falling objects, we can draw conclusions about gravity, as Galileo and Newton did.

Similarly, you can't see or measure the principles behind innate thinking; *they're formless too*. But you can observe and measure their effects. In fact, as you continue deepening your understanding of innate thinking, you're going to start seeing the effects on a daily basis. Just as there are no exceptions to the principle of gravity, there are no exceptions to the principles of innate thinking; they're a constant.

Our mental functioning influences every aspect of our lives on a daily basis. Understanding the principles behind the experience of life gives you massive leverage. The *implications* of these principles are profound for individuals, organizations and entire societies.

DISTINCTION: Applications vs. Implications

Single-paradigm pioneers, Valda Monroe and Keith Blevens, PhD, draw a powerful distinction between **applications** and **implications**.

When we don't understand the principles behind how something works, we tend to look for **applications**. Procedures, "how-tos" and step-by-step processes are an attempt to make progress when we don't intuitively know how something works. The vast majority of personal development, business and leadership books are focused on **applications** in the absence of a principled understanding. As a result, people often have trouble implementing what they've learned from those programmes, and add the **applications** to the list of things they know they "should" be doing.

The principles behind how something works have **implications**. When you intuitively understand these principles, the **implications** inform and guide your thoughts and behaviours in the moment, resolving issues that were previously insoluble and revealing opportunities that were previously invisible.

An example is physical health. Until the middle of the 19th century, there was little or no awareness of germs. The germ theory of disease was developed in the late 1800s before being proved by Robert Koch (a feat which earned him the Nobel Prize in 1905). The world of medicine started changing radically (surgeons started washing their hands, sterilizing their instruments and wearing masks over their nose and mouth while performing surgery). Beyond that, the principles of germ theory had widespread implications for *everyone* who learned about it.

Even a *rudimentary* awareness of principles has implications for your behaviour. While you may only have a basic understanding of germ theory, it's likely that you've learned to wash your hands regularly, cover your mouth when you cough and are careful when handling anything you think is a significant source of germs and bacteria.

The *Innate Thinking*® model is a business-friendly coding of the principles behind our experience, and the implications of those principles. As you continue getting a deeper understanding of innate thinking, you'll start experiencing a gentle yet powerful transformation, with more clarity, resilience and well-being. And why does insightful understanding of these principles make such an impact in people's lives?

Clarity of understanding leads to clarity of mind...

The outside-in misunderstanding – the false assumption that we're feeling something *other than* our thinking in the moment – is the only thing that ever keeps us from clarity. Clear up the misunderstanding, and the mind clears.

The factory settings

Clarity, resilience and peace of mind are the default setting for people; our true nature. They are our natural state when our minds are clear and free from superstitious thinking. As you continue deepening your understanding of innate thinking, you'll start experiencing the "default settings" more of the time. These default settings are the "deep drivers" behind individual and business success.

Deep Driver	Description	What it drives...
Clarity: A clear mind, free from superstitious thinking, fully present and in the moment, with the levels of performance, satisfaction and enjoyment that brings.	The modern business world faces increasing complexity and rapid change while struggling with time scarcity, attention-poverty, information-saturation and communication overwhelm. Clarity is the ability to discern the factors that make a difference and act on them productively, without being distracted by the "noise" in the system.	• High performance • Effective leadership • Presence • Insight • Confidence • Timely decision making • Detecting opportunities • Competitive advantage • Rapid response to change • Dealing with complexity • Productivity • Reduced stress • Increased focus
Direction: A sense of direction, purpose and motivation, free from urgency and undue pressure.	Every enterprise requires a clear sense of direction. A felt connection to a shared vision is a strong predictor of business success, yet it's surprising how often the people in a business have either lost sight of that shared vision, or no longer feel passionately connected to it.	• Authentic leadership • Shared vision and purpose • Focus of resources • Employee engagement • Strategic planning • Brand clarity and passion • Sustainability • Resolves uncertainty • Shared goals • Motivation
Resilience: A strong sense of inner resilience, security and trust in yourself and your world.	Resilience is essential for dealing with the ups and downs of life. It's the deep driver behind why some people (and businesses) bounce back in the face of setbacks, while others struggle to recover. Yet most people in business don't understand where resilience comes from, or how to cultivate it.	• Thriving through uncertainty • Rapid recovery from setbacks • Dealing with change • Responsiveness and flexibility • Confident delivery • Agility and staying power • Mental fitness/toughness

Deep Driver	Description	What it drives...
Creativity: A reliable source of creativity and insight for innovating and solving problems.	Creativity is the driver behind all problem-solving and innovation. Consequently, it's an essential power-source for all businesses. Yet it's often overlooked, or seen as the domain of advertising agencies or other "creatives."	• Soft and hard innovation • Problem-solving • Disruptive strategy • Blue ocean strategy • Product and service design • Customer delight • Market leadership • Brand narrative • Opportunity creation
Connection: Warm, genuine connections with other people, leading to stronger relationships with clients, colleagues, friends, family-members and lovers.	Relationships in a business are a key measure of business strength. Strong relationships with customers result in loyalty. The benefits of strong colleague and supplier relationships are equally evident. Connection is the deep driver behind strong relationships.	• Understanding customer needs • Service culture • Employee engagement • Effective meetings • Productive, agile teams • Collaborative solutions • Contribution and caring • Sustainability • Social marketing • Effective communication • Effective listening • Persuasion and influence • Word of mouth/referrals • Brand loyalty

Deep Driver	Description	What it drives...
Authenticity: The freedom to be who you are, speak your truth and do what you believe to be right.	The rise of social media has put businesses under increasing pressure to demonstrate transparency, integrity and authenticity. This trend is set to continue, and authenticity is the deep driver that will differentiate the companies that "walk the walk" from those who just "talk the talk."	• Authentic leadership • Integrity • Transparency • Customer loyalty • Employee engagement • Brand clarity and passion • Trust and credibility • Raving fans • Differentiation
Intuition: Alignment with your intuition and inner wisdom, your internal guidance system.	Whether you call it intuition, wisdom or "gut feel," business leaders from Richard Branson to Steve Jobs have acknowledged it as one of the key drivers in creating market-leading results. But few businesses understand what it is, how it works and how to develop it.	• Effective decision making • Opportunity spotting • Disruptive offerings • Blue ocean strategy • Market leadership • Soft and hard innovation • Product and service design • Competitive advantage • Sustainability
Presence: Present, aware and available to the moment, connected with your mind, your body and the world around you.	Presence is a rare quality, but when someone has it, other people sit up and take notice. Presence brings with it playful curiosity, charisma and enhanced awareness, making it a particularly attractive and sought-after quality.	• Influencing others • Charismatic leadership • Clear view of reality • Enhanced awareness • Enhanced forecasting • Trend-detection • Opportunity spotting • Natural attractiveness • Embodied learning

Expectation management

While these deep drivers are your birthright, nobody experiences them all the time. Outside-in thinking comes with the territory; we all find ourselves living in a THOUGHT-generated reality before we know THOUGHT has anything to do with it. But you can look at it like the lanes on a motorway; the ability to notice and make adjustments when you're drifting out of your lane is more important (and realistic) than trying to stay in the middle of your lane 100% of the time.

Breaking news!

On 29 August, 2012, I was invited by Sky TV's Breaking News programme to come to the studio and be interviewed live, on-air, watched by over five million people (England's cricket captain, Andrew Strauss, was about to resign, and Sky wanted to get a psychological perspective on his decision).

It was to be my first time being interviewed on the TV news. As I waited offstage in the "green room," I was feeling anxious and nervous (i.e. my head was full of superstitious, outside-in thinking). While I knew on one level that my feelings were coming from my thinking in the moment, they still looked and felt real to me.

Another guest (a seasoned commentator) turned to me and asked how I was doing. I explained, and he asked what I was going to do about it. My reply shocked him. *"Nothing,"* I said. *"I know that if I leave my thinking alone, I'll have what I need when I'm on the air."* I explained that I didn't need to be in a "high-performance state" while I was in the green room, so I wasn't in one. When I was on the air, I'd have what I needed to deliver the goods.

A production assistant came to collect me. My heart was pounding as I walked into the studio and took a seat across from newscaster Dermot Murnaghan but, as he introduced me, my head cleared. I put my attention on listening to his questions as deeply as I could (listening for insight and inspiration) then gave answers that I'm still happy with today.

If I'd tried to use a technique to clear my mind or "get in a good state" while I was in the green room, I would have been interfering with a self-correcting system. But when I allowed my mind to self-correct, I found that I had what I needed when the time came. When you've got nothing on your mind, you're free to give your best.

Context-sensitive

The mind is context-sensitive. The *Innate Thinking®* model points to an extraordinary "intelligence" capable of giving you what you need when you need it. The mindset that's most practical and useful for a job interview isn't necessarily the one that will give you the richest experience of sharing a sunset with your lover. The mindset that's most effective when coming up with a solution to a serious business problem isn't necessarily the one that will help you deliver the goods when you're delivering an inspirational speech to rally the troops.

Having all the resources to deal with the situation at hand is one of the *implications* of a deeper understanding of innate thinking. The more deeply you understand how the system works, the more you get to benefit from the implications of the principles behind it.

Even when we know about them, we all sometimes lose sight of the fact that principles are creating our experience of life. We get caught up in our thinking and slip into the outside-in illusion (the principles are creating *that* experience too!) Fortunately, there's a brilliant system we've each got to let you know when that's happened, and point you back in the direction of your innate thinking…

***keep exploring ⋅⋅⋅ connect with others
share your discoveries ⋅⋅⋅ deepen your understanding***

Reflection point: *I invite you to open to the possibility that the qualities people prize most highly (clarity, creativity, love, peace, presence and freedom, to name just a few) are traits you already possess. How surprised would you be if you were to suddenly realize these qualities are your natural state when there's nothing else in the way?*

There's something both surprising and familiar about catching a glimpse of the default settings of your true nature. You may recognize some of the "deep drivers" in yourself very easily, while others may seem a little more elusive. They're all part of who you are. Take a moment now to share what you're discovering by scanning the QR code with your smartphone or type the URL below into your browser. It's a good way to document your thoughts about what's making a difference to you. It can also be useful to have a look at some of the discoveries other people are sharing since reading this chapter...

www.ClarityBook.biz/chapter4

5

The Psychological Immune System

....

"The major problems in the world are the result of the difference between how nature works and the way people think."

Gregory Bateson, Epistemologist

"You're feeling your *thinking*, not what you're thinking *about*..."

My friend looked bemused by my statement. He wanted me to cure his fear of flying, so I started by asking how he knew when to start becoming afraid, and how he knew when to stop. He told me that it usually started a week before his flight, and dissipated 20 or 30 minutes later.

"I've got some great news for you," I told him. *"You're not afraid of flying!"*

"I'm not?" he asked in surprise.

"No," I replied. *"You have fearful **thinking** around flying."*

"Isn't that the same thing?" he responded, dubiously.

"No, it isn't the same thing," I said. *"You're feeling your **thinking**, not what you're thinking **about**..."*

People are notoriously bad at predicting their felt response to imagined scenarios. David is sure he'll fall apart if he gets made redundant, but it turns out to be one of the best things that's ever happened to him. Jennifer is convinced that her job is the source of all her woes, but when she gets a new one, her woes come along for the ride. Michael is excited about starting a business, sure he's going to love it, but he ends up struggling with stress and disillusionment. Jennifer has massive self-doubt but starts her new venture anyway. As she begins making progress, she blossoms and thrives.

And why are we so bad at these predictions?

Because we're feeling our *thinking*, not what we're thinking *about*.

The brilliance of the body

Our bodies and minds have developed over millions of years to survive and thrive in a world full of threats and opportunities. We are born with a powerful immune system that protects us from illness and disease. The immune system reflects an innate tendency towards health and wellness that also shows up in the body's ability to repair wounds, breaks and other injuries. Even something as simple as a cut, scratch or scrape initiates a "wound healing cascade," an intricate series of processes that automatically protect the injured area, remove dead tissue, regenerate new cells and heal the injury-site.

We also have built-in systems to save our lives in the presence of danger. Fear is a powerful survival signal, an intense feeling of distress and alarm that can be used to alert us to a danger in our immediate environment, and move us to take action; fight, flight or freeze. The purpose of fear is to keep us alive, and to protect us from dangerous situations. If you're sitting in Starbucks and a hungry tiger saunters through the front door, fear can be a powerful evolutionary gift that saves your life.

You might attribute these powers to a biological life-force, to a creative intelligence, to the awesome engine of evolution, or to random chance. Whether you attribute them to all four or to none of the above, the fact remains: they're extraordinary abilities.

All of this happens without any conscious intervention from the owner (you). You don't have to think about it. In fact, most of the repair and regeneration your body has done in your lifetime has taken place without you even being aware of it. Your natural instinct to recoil from a hot flame or put your hands up to protect against a blow are expressions of the same deeper tendency towards health, wellness and survival. But there's something you may not have realized until now...

You also have a psychological immune system...

Just as we each receive pain signals to let us know when our physical well-being is under threat, we also receive signals that "wake us up" when our heads are filling up with superstitious thinking.

The tip of the iceberg

The portion of an iceberg that's visible above the water's surface typically only represents 11% of the iceberg's total volume. Looking at the tip doesn't tell you anything about the shape of the submerged portion of the iceberg.

Our moment-to-moment thinking is like an iceberg...

We live in a THOUGHT-generated experiential reality; 100% of our experience is coming from 100% of our thinking in the moment. But the individual thoughts that we notice going through our minds (i.e. what we're thinking *about*) are like the tip of the iceberg; they only comprise a tiny portion of the thinking that's creating our experience of the moment. Like the submerged portion of the iceberg, the majority of our thinking is invisible.

So how do you know what's in the invisible portion of your thinking? Your feelings. Feeling and thinking are like two sides of the same coin. Your feelings are the *visible face* of your (invisible) thinking.

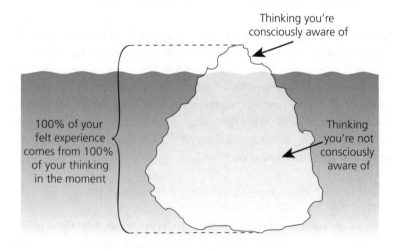

Figure 5.1. The Thinking/Feeling Iceberg

Reality Check

Some people object, *"Are you seriously trying to tell me that getting punched doesn't hurt unless you think it does?"*

No, I'm not saying that. But 100% of your *experience* of a punch (or anything else) comes to you via THOUGHT, the reality principle. You never feel anything that isn't in your thinking. There are plenty of everyday examples of this fact:

- *The scratch, bruise or cut that you don't discover until minutes or hours after it happens. It wasn't in your thinking when it happened, so you didn't feel it.*

- *The problem that you dwell on and worry about all day, then forget about entirely while watching a particularly engaging film that evening. Something else is in your thinking, so you don't experience the problem.*

- *The lamppost you walk into as you're thinking about something else. The lamppost isn't in your thinking until you walk into it; then it is in your thinking!*

So what does this have to do with clarity?

When we believe we're feeling something *other than* our thinking, our minds fill up and speed up. The more superstitious thinking is in our minds, the less clarity we experience. The less superstitious thinking is in our minds, the more clarity we experience. When you're experiencing a high degree of clarity, you're not thinking about anything; you've got nothing on your mind. This is sometimes described as "flow."

Fearful thinking

If flying was genuinely the cause of my friend's anxiety, he would be at his most frightened when the plane was in the air, and it wouldn't start diminishing until after the plane had landed. The fact that he spent the major portion of the flight feeling fine meant that he wasn't afraid of flying; he was experiencing something else entirely.

International disasters such as the 9/11 World Trade Centre attacks, the explosion of the space shuttle *Challenger*, and the more recent BP Gulf oil rig disaster all have one thing in common: in every case, the official investigations reported that early warning signs were either ignored or misinterpreted. The fact is that, no matter how clear a signal is...

A signal is only as good as your understanding of it...

Thought Experiment

Imagine a malicious driving instructor who teaches a new driver that a green traffic light means "stop" and a red light means "go." If the learner ever tried to drive through a city, there would be chaos! The traffic signals would be working perfectly well, but the driver's misunderstanding of the signals would likely lead to a collision. While this example is as unlikely as it is absurd, it raises two important points:

1. *Misunderstanding of valid signals can lead to extreme difficulties.*

2. *All it takes to solve a misunderstanding is insightful understanding.*

How to recover from a tailspin

In the early days of aviation, a pilot's worst enemy was the tailspin. Planes would unexpectedly go into a rapid, spinning descent that typically ended in a fatal crash.

If a plane went into a spin, the pilot's impulse (based on their training and experience of flying under normal conditions) was to pull back on the stick, but this only served to make a tailspin worse. For years, it was common knowledge that if a pilot was unlucky enough to find themselves in a tailspin, they were doomed.

In 1912, Lieutenant Wilfred Parke went into an accidental tailspin at 700 feet while flying his biplane. Parke pulled back on the stick, but the plane continued its terrifying death-plunge. Then, with only seconds to live, Parke did something utterly counterintuitive; he applied full right rudder. Onlookers watched in amazement as the doomed aircraft suddenly levelled out at 50 feet. Lieutenant Parke had just discovered how to get out of a tailspin!

"Parke's Technique" was revealed in 1912, but pilots continued to die because of their impulse to pull back on the stick if they went into a spin. They "understood it intellectually," but they didn't have the insightful/embodied understanding that would save their lives. It wasn't until 1914, at the start of World War I, that pilots started receiving the training that would allow them to practice tailspin recovery. Experiencing it for themselves under controlled conditions gave them the insightful understanding that would save their lives if they ever went into an accidental tailspin.

The trick is not minding that it hurts

In a famous scene from the classic film *Lawrence of Arabia* (Horizon Pictures, 1962), T.E. Lawrence (played by Peter O'Toole) slowly extinguishes a burning match between his thumb and forefinger while his men look on in amazement. One of the men, William Potter, tries to replicate the feat, but recoils in pain...

Potter: "Ooh! It damn well hurts!"

Lawrence: "Certainly it hurts."

Potter: "Well what's the trick then?"

Lawrence: "The trick, William Potter, is not minding that it hurts."

The pain withdrawal reflex is an involuntary response that moves your body (or part of your body) away from a source of pain. If you've ever accidentally touched a candle flame or a hot stove, you've experienced the pain withdrawal reflex. While the response is involuntary (i.e. not under your conscious control), it's still mediated by THOUGHT. A person who is under the influence of drink or drugs will not always exhibit the response, and people can actually be conditioned to override it (as Lawrence did).

The mental equivalent of the pain withdrawal reflex is most clearly exhibited in children under five years old. Toddlers can go from excruciating mental torment one minute to laughing and giggling the next. Even the most extreme tantrum doesn't last for long in the big scheme of things; certainly not as long as most adults' bouts of superstitious thinking.

A little child will only go so far into painful thinking, and only stay there so long before the "mental pain withdrawal reflex" kicks in and guides them back to clarity. The psychological immune system takes care of their mental well-being just as the physical immune system takes care of their physical well-being. So why isn't this response so obvious in teenagers and adults?

People can be conditioned to override it...

The natural system we have for guiding us out of painful superstitious thinking gets overridden by our conditioning. So if we've been conditioned out of it, how do we "wake up" when we're lost in thought?

We are all born with a fully functioning psychological immune system; mentally ill infants are few and far between. But as we grow up, we get conditioned into thought-habits of our family and our culture; thought-habits that include the outside-in misunderstanding. Some people are less conditioned by it than others; you probably know people who seem to be unusually resilient and philosophical in the face of hardship and crisis, just as you know others who seem to fall apart at the slightest provocation. The variable is this:

*People who seem to fall apart at the slightest provocation
are convinced that their thinking is real. People who are resilient
and resourceful in the face of hardship and crisis
intuitively know their thinking is an illusion...*

So how do you begin to "see through" this conditioning? Insightful understanding. As you continue reading this book and deepening your understanding of innate thinking, you'll start to notice stale habits of superstitious thinking dropping away, and clarity emerging to take their place.

Here's a familiar example...

From time to time I get annoyed with someone. If I'm mildly annoyed, I typically have some flexibility of perspective; perhaps I didn't express myself clearly enough, or maybe they got the wrong end of the stick. When mildly annoyed, I tend to give people "the benefit of the doubt" and cut them some slack. Why? Because in those moments, I'm able to take a philosophical view and see that there are many ways of looking at a situation. I may even find myself laughing at my annoyance, intuitively knowing that I'm not seeing clearly. I recognize that my superstitious thinking is clouding my judgement at the moment, even though it looks clear to me that the other person is in the wrong. As a result, my psychological immune system can guide me back to clarity.

But it's different when I'm *really* angry. Then, I'm convinced that I'm right; that there's only one way of looking at the situation and it's my way. The more agitated I feel, the more "right" my thinking looks. I'm hypnotized by my superstitious thoughts (the idea that my feelings of anger are coming from somewhere *other than* my thinking). In those moments, I used to interpret the strength of my agitated feelings as a sign that my perceptions were accurate. In fact, I still sometimes do, but these days there's a difference. Now if I become very angry, I'll rant and rage for a while before it occurs to me that I'm feeling my thinking. While I may still be angry, the insight that I'm feeling my thinking does something for me; it's the start of an automatic, innate process guiding me back to clarity. The self-correcting system is doing its job.

Reality Check

"Are you saying that anger is bad; that all anger is unhelpful thinking?" No! I'm suggesting that anger (and every other emotion) is a case of feeling your *thinking*, not what you're thinking *about*.

Remember: the mind is context-sensitive. *Innate Thinking®* points to an extraordinary "intelligence" capable of giving you what you need when you need it. Anger is part of the rich palette of human emotions; fit for purpose in certain situations and totally unhelpful in others.

You may well find yourself in situations where anger is an entirely appropriate and useful emotion; your inner wisdom giving you what you need to deal with the circumstances at hand. If you can see that you're feeling your thinking in those moments, you'll have the clarity of mind to deal effectively with the situation, using the anger for the purpose it was intended. However, when we believe the anger is coming from somewhere *other than* our thinking, we can be a danger to ourselves and others. This simple misunderstanding is the cause of countless workplace conflicts and broken relationships.

Rumble strips

On motorways, highways and autobahns all over the world, rumble strips along the side of the road alert drivers who are travelling too near the edge. The signal is simple and well understood: they've started to go off-track. The moment a driver starts feeling the rumble, they correct their course easily.

We all drift off the road into superstitious thinking; it's part of our experience. But as you start to see through the outside-in misunderstanding, something changes. At some point when you start to go off track, it will occur to you that your feelings are coming from your thinking in the moment. This is the start of your psychological immune system's self-correcting process. You don't need to do anything to help it along; the process of self-correction is an automatic function of your mind.

And everyone has it!

So if everyone has this powerful and elegant system built into them, why do so many people spend so much of their time riding on the rumble strips? If everyone's got this natural ability to find their clarity and wisdom, why is there so much stress, pressure and conflict? So much crime, divorce, addiction and war? If everyone has an innate guidance system for keeping them on track, why does it so often seem like they're not using it?

---

keep exploring ❖ connect with others
share your discoveries ❖ deepen your understanding

Reflection point: *"The major problems in the world are the result of the difference between how nature works and the way people think." Take a moment or two to reflect on Gregory Bateson's statement. By definition, it must apply to the problems of business, of relationships, of our personal struggles. Could it really be this simple?*

We are the spearhead of evolution; the result of countless millennia of trial and error. Our understanding of the nature of THOUGHT is our biggest leverage point for making progress. For more *Clarity* resources relating to Chapter 5 – The Psychological Immune System, scan the QR code with your smartphone or type the URL below into your browser. As you explore the materials, experiment with trusting your intuition about what to comment on and share with others…

www.ClarityBook.biz/chapter5

6

Habitual Thought Patterns

"What the thinker thinks, the prover proves."

Leonard Orr, Writer
and philosopher

"It took a long time for my thinking to get this messed up, so it's going to take a long time for it to get sorted out..."

Everyone nodded in agreement. It seemed to make sense. The phrase was one I'd heard countless times during my recovery from alcoholism, and its speakers had a positive intention; to acknowledge the (sometimes slow) learning and growing process of recovery, in contrast to the "instant fix" of drugs, alcohol and other substances.

But this simple piece of "received wisdom" also reveals a basic confusion people tend to have when it comes to the mind.

People tend to think, speak and act as though their thoughts have the same qualities as the material world...

Look at the following phrases:

- "The company's issues are really deep-rooted. They won't be easy to resolve."

- "This is a really big problem. It's going to be tough for our team to sort it out."

- "It took a long time for my thinking to get this messed up, so it's going to take a long time for it to get sorted out."

Each of these phrases has at least one example of the speaker attributing qualities from the *material* world to their thinking:

Phrase	False Implication	Reality
"The company's issues are really deep-rooted. They won't be easy to resolve."	Issues have *roots*, and some *roots* are *deeper* than others. And of course, the *deeper* the *roots* are, the less easy the issues are to resolve.	Issues are thoughts. The idea that issues have roots is also a thought. The idea that roots have depth and the deeper they are, the trickier that makes them to resolve is also a thought. All these thoughts are made of THOUGHT, a formless energy, so they're not subject to the laws of the material world. There are countless examples of "deep-rooted" issues that have been resolved quickly and easily. Especially when a person understands the nature of THOUGHT.
"This is a really big problem. It's going to be tough for our team to sort it out."	There are these things called *problems*, they come in different *sizes* (small, medium, large), and they need to be *sorted out*. The *bigger* they are, the more *difficult* they are to *sort out*.	When a person or group perceives something as a problem, it means they've got thinking that they're labelling "problem." Whether large or small, it's all thinking. When a person has an insight, their thinking (which may have looked like a big problem five minutes ago) is suddenly "sorted out," even though they didn't do anything to sort it out.
"It took a long time for my thinking to get this messed up, so it's going to take a long time for it to get sorted out."	*Messy thinking* is like a messy office or a garden that hasn't been cared for. The more *time* that elapses as it gets messy, the more *time* (and effort) it's going to take to *sort it out*. Like some enormous warehouse full of stuff, the more time spent on making it messy, the longer it takes to tidy it up.	THOUGHT is a creative energy, and the thought-forms we create using it have no substance; they're literally made of "the stuff that dreams are made of." Have you ever noticed how fleeting dreams can be? How one minute you're experiencing a rich dreamscape, and the next minute you're wide awake and having trouble remembering what the dream was about? The dream is so fleeting because it's made of THOUGHT. And your thinking is made of the same thing. It can change instantly the moment you have an insight. Time is a function of the material world, but THOUGHT isn't subject to the laws of the material world. People can experience a moment of clarity, and see a situation (or their lives) change in a matter of moments.

*We all intuitively know that our thoughts
are fleeting and ephemeral...*

That's why we write down phone numbers, notes and to-do lists; because we recognize that if we don't write it down before we go to the shops, it may be gone when we next look for it. Yet we don't seem to remember that fact in other areas of our lives.

What the thinker thinks, the prover proves

Leonard Orr summed it up nicely when he explained that you can model the mind as having two key functions: a thinker and a prover. The thinker can think absolutely anything:

- The world is flat/round/spherical.
- People are wonderful/nasty/only human.
- Life is hard/easy/a bowl of cherries.
- Change is a struggle/natural/effortless.

The thinker has infinite flexibility, but the prover has a much simpler job; what the thinker thinks, the prover proves:

- If you think this book is boring, then you'll experience it as boring.
- If you think this book is fascinating, then you'll experience it as fascinating.

Remember: THOUGHT is the best special effects department in the world, powered by MIND and brought to life in our experience by CONSCIOUSNESS. Our thinking always looks real. Our THOUGHT-generated experiential reality looks like an *actual* reality, but it's not. We're each living in the feeling of our thinking, moment to moment; an experience that's generated by the principles of innate thinking.

So, if we each have innate clarity and resilience, and our thinking is just "the stuff that dreams are made of," why are so many people in thrall to their habitual thinking? Why are the plagues of stress, pressure, addiction, greed and hostility wreaking such havoc in the world? If little children demonstrate the characteristics of clarity – presence, joy, creativity, connection, resilience etc. – why is that so often NOT the case in older children, teenagers and adults?

There are several reasons…

1 Little children know they don't really understand how life works. They haven't bought into a "game plan for living"; a set of rules that they have to try and fit themselves into. They intuitively know that their understanding of how life works is incomplete, and subject to revision at any time.

2 As a result, little children have comparatively little habitual thinking. Their experience of life is largely uncluttered by their cognitive models. The perceptual channels that allow a person to deeply experience the richness of life haven't been clogged up with habits of superstitious thinking.

3 Consequently, little children haven't yet learned that there's anything wrong with thinking whatever they think, and feeling whatever they feel. They're not trying to correct their thinking, or trying to change their feelings. When they feel angry, frightened or sad, they're fully committed to it, and when it's over, it's over. They feel whatever they feel, then allow themselves to return to clarity.

4 Plus, they have an intuitive feel for the illusory and transitory nature of thoughts. They haven't been conditioned out of the psychological equivalent of the pain withdrawal response.

Of course, as children grow up, the self-correcting quality of their minds does get paved over by conditioning. They create habitual patterns of superstitious thinking, and relate to those patterns as a reality.

Medication time... medication time...

I started drinking alcohol when I was 12 years old. By the time I was 20, I was what's referred to as a "high-functioning alcoholic." I loved the feeling of peace, freedom and aliveness that alcohol gave me. But I was deeply troubled by the effects it had on my life, and the lives of those around me. I tried to control my drinking, but every attempt at control eventually resulted in greater chaos. By the time I was 30, I was done. I had a moment of clarity, and decided to stop drinking. But things went from bad to worse. After nine months without a drink, I was depressed and suicidal. My habitual patterns of superstitious thinking were robbing my life of any sense of peace, joy or aliveness. So I decided to get help.

Over the past 16 years, I've come to see the alcoholic's drinking, the drug addict's using, and every other addict's seemingly pathological behaviour, as an example of medicating. And what is the addict trying to medicate?

Their habitual patterns of superstitious thinking.

The addict's use of drink/drugs/sex/shopping/gambling is an "intervention" that offers temporary relief from their habitual patterns of superstitious thinking, and the painful feelings that often accompany them.

Remember: Many of the biggest disasters of the last few decades were the result of misinterpretation; valid signals that weren't properly understood.

Similarly, many of the behavioural problems people experience (ranging from distraction to addiction) are the result of an attempt to medicate agitated, uncomfortable feelings that look like they're coming from something *other than* their thinking.

Our habitual superstitious thinking (and the feelings that accompany it) is all that ever stands between us and the high levels of clarity, security and peace of mind we all have inside.

The river still flows

Imagine a river that starts to cool as winter comes. As the temperature falls, ice crystals begin to form along the riverbanks. As it keeps getting colder, the ice crystals start forming small blocks of ice that break free of the banks and flow down the river. At various points the blocks of ice cluster together, and the river begins to freeze over. Eventually, the surface of the river is a solid sheet of ice. But all the while, just beneath the surface, the river still flows.

Our habits of superstitious thinking are like the ice on the surface of the river; the only thing that ever stands in the way of clarity, and a rich experience of life. But beneath that seemingly solid mass, the river still flows. Just as the ice was created from flowing water, our habits of superstitious thinking are created from THOUGHT, the formless energy behind our experience of life.

And behind all our superstitious thinking, the endless river of THOUGHT is still flowing, carrying the powerful resources of innate clarity, resilience and well-being to the surface of our awareness; bringing fresh new thinking to solve our problems and create new possibilities.

When we're locked in a mind-made prison of habitual thoughts, it seems ludicrous to think that freedom could be so nearby. At least, until you realize who has the key...

**keep exploring ⁘ connect with others
share your discoveries ⁘ deepen your understanding**

Reflection point: While we all have material challenges to deal with from time to time, what turns them into insoluble problems is our thinking. If we were to interview 1000 people with serious mental health issues, they would all likely be convinced that their thinking is real. In fact, the majority of problems we all have are grounded in the mistaken belief that our thinking is real. Reflect on this for a few moments. Is it possible that many of the things you've been experiencing as problems until now are a reflection of the spurious belief that your thinking was real?

Once you've reflected on this, take a few moments to share your discoveries online, as well as any questions you may have about this curious phenomenon. When you scan the QR code with your smartphone or type the URL below into your browser, you'll find more great *Clarity* resources relating to this subject. As you share your discoveries and keep connecting with other people around their insights and a-has, you'll notice your clarity of understanding continuing to increase…

www.ClarityBook.biz/chapter6

7

Stress: The Source and the Solution

··

"You're always living in the feeling of your thinking."

Keith Blevens, Clinical psychologist

"What are you looking for?"

The time was 2 a.m. The policeman had just walked round the corner to find a dishevelled-looking man on his hands and knees, searching frantically beneath a streetlight.

"I'm looking for my key," the man replied, obviously intoxicated.

"Where did you lose it?" the police officer inquired.

"I dropped it in the long grass on a vacant lot, a couple of blocks away," said the man, still searching.

"Then why are you looking here?" asked the puzzled cop.

The man rolled his eyes, then spoke slowly, as if explaining something to a small child…

"Because the light's better here."

The man's mistake in this Sufi joke is so obvious as to be ridiculous, but there are times when we are all that drunken seeker. Each one of us is searching under a streetlight for the key that isn't there when we're looking to something *other than* our thinking for the security/resilience/well-being/creativity/confidence/connection/fulfilment/success we desire.

We don't walk around in our *circumstances*; we walk around in our *experience*. Everything in our experience is created using Thought, the reality principle. Our experience of the world "out there" is Thought-generated. Your perception is an illusion; a practical and compelling one, but an illusion nevertheless.

The source of stress

So what does this have to do with stress? Here's what:

*The true source of stress is the mistaken
belief that we're feeling something other
than THOUGHT taking form in the moment...
... that we're at the mercy of something other
than our thinking; a world "out there"
in space or time with power
over how we feel...*

THOUGHT is the *formless* energy that creates the *form* of our moment-to-moment experience. Just as sand can be used to make any kind of sandcastle or sand sculpture, THOUGHT can create any kind of perceptual form.

The table overleaf shows how it works. For clarity of understanding, I've laid this out *sequentially over time*, but in reality it all happens *simultaneously* and *instantaneously*. THOUGHT creates an entire experiential reality in an instant; we're *in it* before we realize THOUGHT has anything to do with it.

In Chapter 4, I explained that misdirection is the initiation of a train of thought based on a false assumption. The moment we believe our felt experience is coming from something *other than* thinking in the moment, we've accepted a false assumption and climbed aboard. This is the inevitable result of believing that thinking and feeling are separate; they're not. Thinking and feeling are two sides of the same coin. Which means...

*We're never stressed out about what we
think we're stressed out about...*

*We're only ever stressed out because we believe we're feeling
something other than thinking in the moment...*

How stress works

When we believe our agitated, unpleasant feelings are coming from
something *other than* THOUGHT taking form in the moment
(e.g. money, other people, the past, the future, health, etc.)...

We automatically assume something *other than*
thinking has power over our felt experience

Which puts us at the mercy of that *"something other than our thinking"*
and thrusts us into the position of "victim"...

Making it essential that we control/manage/manipulate that
"something other than our thinking" in order to protect/
guarantee our felt experience, now and in the future...

So our heads fill up with superstitious thinking, a "to-do list"
of management tactics sponsored by this mistaken belief...

And because we're always feeling our thinking, we have
a felt experience of this "troubling" world, where *"something other than
our thinking"* has power over how we feel...

Resulting in a congested, speedy mind...
insecurity, neediness and isolation...
stress, worry and anxiety...
etc.

The belief that we're feeling something other than our thinking
turns us into victims. Some people respond to that by retreating,
defending or manipulating, while others come out fighting; either

way, they're responding to an illusion. Of course, this doesn't just apply to stress; everything from worry and anxiety to anger and rage can be the result of this subtle but catastrophic misdirection.

And, strange as it may seem, it can also apply to pleasant experiences. The idea that our fun/happy/enjoyable/exciting/loving feelings are coming from something other than THOUGHT in the moment is equally misguided; it just doesn't work that way.

Reality Check

Some people worry that life would be flat, dull and boring if they were to realize their felt experience is always coming from their thinking, but nothing could be further from the truth.

Once a person has a realization about the nature of films, they're able to enjoy films *more*. We can still engage deeply with a film, being touched and moved, even though we understand how films work. The fact that we know our security isn't at risk allows us to enter more deeply into the experience.

In the same way, as you continue learning about the workings of innate thinking, you'll find yourself entering more deeply into the experience of life.

We're always and only feeling our thinking in the moment. Period.

*It only works one way. Even when it looks like we're feeling
something other than THOUGHT in the moment,
it still only works one way...*

As mentioned previously, the principles behind innate thinking are *formless*. Before we delve into the "solution" to stress, it's worth exploring what *formless* means.

DISTINCTION: Form vs. Formless

The THOUGHT-generated experiential realities we each occupy contain the **form** of life; the sights, sounds, smells, tastes and feelings that make up our inner and outer worlds. As tangible as it seems, our experience of the **form** of life is actually a mind-made illusion (brought to you by THOUGHT, the best special-effects department there is).

The *power* of THOUGHT, on the other hand, is **formless** by its very nature. Being **formless**, it can take any **form**. You can think of it as the *ability* to create a perceptual **form**.

The intellect is like a filing system for organizing and manipulating forms. But the intellect is utterly incapable of "grasping" something formless. Example: imagine a formless energy. What does it look like? Most people give answers like "A beam of light," "Lightning" or "A cloud," but these are all forms.

DISTINCTION: Tangible vs. Real

When you insert a DVD into a DVD-player and start watching the film it's carrying, something remarkable happens: the digital information encoded on the shiny disc is translated into a set of instructions that are relayed to the TV set, and a dance of electrons appears on the screen. As you watch the TV, you transform that dance of electrons into an experience involving characters, plotline and action.

And it happens so fast, you don't even realize you're doing it...

We don't realize that we're experiencing an illusion as though it were a reality. We don't realize that we're breathing life into the dance of electrons, and creating the relationships between the TV characters. The drama unfolding on the screen is not **real**; it's an illusion that we bring to life with our minds. It's **tangible**, but not **real**.

Compared to the images on the screen, the information encoded on the DVD is relatively **intangible**. You can't tell anything about the movie by looking at the silver spirals on the DVD. But the information on the DVD is giving rise to the drama. In that sense, it's more **real** than our experience of what's on the screen. After all, the DVD could be used to play the movie on thousands of screens simultaneously.

Our felt experience of life is a **tangible** illusion; **tangible**, but not **real**. The formless principles that create our experience are **real**, but not **tangible**. Our experience of life is in the form, but the power behind life is in the formless.

The light's better here

We innocently look in the tangible (but illusory) world of form for our clarity, well-being, security and success because the light's so much better here. But you can never find something where it isn't, no matter how hard you look. Our experience of the world of form is an illusion; an often-practical illusion, but an illusion nevertheless.

Your felt experience doesn't come from the illusion…
Your felt experience comes from what's creating the illusion…

It comes from the principles of innate thinking
that are creating 100% of your experience of reality…

Because the intellect is a form-manipulation system, and cannot conceive of the formless, we need to use metaphors to point to it. The words THOUGHT, CONSCIOUSNESS and MIND are themselves metaphors that point to the formless principles creating our experience of life.

As we go through life, we experience the form of our inner and outer worlds. The formless principles behind innate thinking are what's *creating* that experience.

So what does this have to do with stress? And with clarity?

Road rage

A survey of Britons conducted by Gillette in 2010 found that people listed work, job interviews and traffic as the top three causes of stress. So let's imagine someone who has "stressful work" that they plan to quit, and is stuck in traffic on the way to the job interview for a position they want (we'll call our job-applicant "Jeremy"). For some reason, Jeremy doesn't know how to feel stressed about traffic, so we decide to teach him.

(I've laid this out *sequentially over time* for ease of explanation, but in reality it all happens *simultaneously* and *instantaneously*. THOUGHT creates an entire experiential reality in an instant; we're *in it* before we realize THOUGHT has anything to do with it.)

First, we tell Jeremy to think about the traffic, and to start making thought-forms; mental objects representing what traffic means to him; the causes and the consequences. We tell Jeremy to think about arriving late for the job interview, and to imagine being stuck in his current job forever. We tell him to imagine that the other road-users are deliberately trying to sabotage him, and that vengeful engineers have rigged the traffic lights against him. Most importantly, we tell him to imagine that his security, happiness and peace of mind is at the mercy of these external factors. If Jeremy follows our instructions, his head should fill up with superstitious thinking, and he should start feeling tense, anxious and ill-at-ease. Finally, we tell him to imagine that the traffic is "causing" those feelings. Voila! We've just taught him how to have "traffic stress." If he's *really* good at it, he might even be able to do road rage. (Once again, this doesn't actually happen sequentially; it happens simultaneously in an instant.)

We're always feeling our thinking in the moment.
But when we believe we're feeling something other than thinking,
then it looks like we're feeling what we're thinking about.

It's not that the job interview doesn't matter, or that the traffic isn't inconvenient; the issue is that when we're lost in superstitious thinking, we're not nearly as resilient, resourceful and creative as we could be. Sitting in a traffic jam with clarity, Jeremy might think to change his route or ring ahead and reschedule the interview. With clarity, he might even have found himself leaving early and avoiding the traffic in the first place.

The solution to stress

When we're lost in superstitious thinking, we tend to be obsessed with the "forms" of life. But, as clarity emerges, the forms don't appear to be important in the same way. Athletes often report that when they're in the zone, it seems as though, on the one hand, it doesn't matter whether they win or lose and, on the other hand, they're going to give it all they've got.

This doesn't even make sense as an intellectual construct, but as clarity emerges, it becomes self-evident. We naturally tend to be less concerned with the form of our thinking, and more aligned with the innate thinking that's creating our thoughts; a direction that's accompanied by a deeper felt experience of life, and a sense of well-being.

While we don't all have the words to describe it, every single one of us has experienced it. For one person it may be when they're walking through the woods or looking out at the waves on the ocean; for another person it may be when they're deeply involved in an activity like dancing or running. Sometimes, these moments of deeper connection find us "out of the blue." But they all share something in common...

When we have clarity and peace of mind, it's not personal. We don't tend to be caught up in the form of our superstitious, "it's all about me" thinking. Situations which may have seemed infuriating are suddenly no longer an issue. We "just know" that things will turn out alright.

This deeper, more connected sense is a signal that you're looking away from the form of your thoughts, and are more aligned with what's creating them; the formless principles of innate thinking. An understanding of the formless can be seen in a variety of domains, and goes by many names:

- The no-thing (Buddhism)
- The implicate order (Bohmian physics)
- Life energy (some biologists)
- Spirit (spirituality)
- The great spirit (North American Indians)

Many names, but one direction; looking beyond our experience of the *form* of life to where that experience is coming from.

So what's the "solution" to stress? Insightful understanding of the inside-out nature of life. The moment we insightfully see that 100% of our feeling is coming from THOUGHT in the moment (and not from anything other than that), feelings of stress start diminishing and clarity starts emerging. This doesn't make us "immune" to stress – we still get hoodwinked by superstitious thinking from time to time. But as you continue exploring *Innate Thinking®*, you'll begin to notice your stress levels decreasing in general, and that you have a very different response to many things which used to "stress you out."

And why is "insightful understanding" likely to succeed in a world where the prevailing psychological paradigm identifies an increasing number of different mental disorders every year? Where governments throw their hands up in despair at the rise in addictions, depression and stress? Where businesses are paralyzed in the face of disruptive competitors and increasing complexity? Where individuals battle with attention-poverty, time-scarcity and information-overload?

The answer to all these questions is to be found in a newly discovered leverage point for transformation...

keep exploring ⁖ connect with others
share your discoveries ⁖ deepen your understanding

Reflection point: What would it mean to you (and for you) if you were to suddenly realize that 100% of your felt experience is coming from THOUGHT in the moment? That 0% of your feeling is coming from anywhere other than THOUGHT?

This powerful realization can occur to you at any point. While we all get hoodwinked by the outside-in misunderstanding, your wisdom will wake you up, bringing you back to clarity. Once you've taken some time to reflect, I encourage you to make use of the extra *Clarity* resources for this chapter. Simply scan the QR code with your smartphone or type the URL below into your browser to keep exploring, connecting and sharing what you're learning...

www.ClarityBook.biz/chapter7

8

The Ultimate Leverage Point

"The historian of science may be tempted to exclaim that when paradigms change, the world itself changes with them."

Thomas Kuhn, Physicist,
historian and philosopher
of science

"Pay no attention to that man behind the curtain. Go – before I lose my temper! The Great and Powerful Oz has spoken…"

When I was a little boy, I loved the film *The Wizard of Oz*, but I was frightened of the Wicked Witch of the West, and terrified of her flying monkeys. I would hide behind the sofa when they appeared on the screen. On some level, I didn't understand that those monkeys were just people in costumes, and that even if they really *were* flying monkeys, they couldn't escape from the television screen.

I didn't understand the nature of film.

And I'm not alone. A little over a century ago, in 1896, the Lumière brothers showed a motion picture in public for the first time in history. The film was a 90-second clip of a train arriving at a station, and showed the train moving towards the camera. The audience were excited to be part of this "cinematic first" but, when the film started playing, many of them ran screaming from their seats.

They didn't understand the nature of film.

They didn't realize that there was no way that the train could escape from the screen and plunge into the audience. They saw patterns of light moving on a screen, and responded to a THOUGHT-generated illusion as though it was a material reality.

Hallucinations

One of my first ever coaching clients had a dog phobia. I asked her "How do you know when to get frightened?" Her head shot back, and she said "As soon as I see the gnashing jaws," while using her hands to mimic a dog snapping at her face. When she saw a dog, even if it was 50 feet away and on a lead, she would generate this frightening hallucination and respond accordingly.

She was responding to a THOUGHT-generated illusion as though it was a material reality.

It's easy to laugh at the Lumière brothers' audience, or to dismiss my dog-phobic client's fear as "irrational," but each of us gets hypnotized by the same order of illusion on a daily basis. Whether a person is worrying or daydreaming; stressing out because they're stuck in traffic or getting excited about a date they're going on later; they're experiencing a THOUGHT-generated experiential reality.

So what has this got to do with clarity?

Increasing clarity is the inevitable result
of a transformation in your understanding
of how life works, and your becoming
more aligned with reality...

When it comes to people changing, there are four "levels" where a person can get leverage.

Level 1 – Material reality

The material world is bound by certain laws, such as gravity. If a person drops a brick on their foot, it will likely do some damage. If a person exercises regularly, their muscles will get stronger. If a train is coming towards you, get out of the way. The yellow lines at the edge of the platform are there for a reason.

Level 2 – The content of thinking (i.e. what you're thinking *about*)

Sigmund Freud popularized the idea that the content of a person's thinking (particularly so-called repressed memories) "caused" their current experience. He thought that if a person could understand what had happened to them in the past, and why they did what they did, this understanding would free them from mental torment and unhelpful behaviours. Millions of people have spent countless years in psychoanalysis in the (often vain) hope that an intellectual understanding would make a practical difference to their lives.

Making changes at this level is like changing the content of a movie (or making up stories about the impact of movies you watched in the past). If a person doesn't understand the nature of movies, and is frightened by what's on the screen, one option is to change the content to something that doesn't frighten them (e.g. rabbits, mittens or cake). This is one of the reasons why it's a good idea for parents to carefully choose the films and TV programmes they let young children watch; because little kids often don't really understand the nature of film... until they do!

Level 3 – The structure of thinking

In the early 1970s, the originators of neuro-linguistic programming (NLP) modelled some of the finest change-workers of the day, and came to the conclusion that the *structure* of a person's thinking was playing a significant role in shaping their experience. They found that altering the *structure* of a person's thinking often had a bigger impact on their experience and behaviour than exploring the *content* of their thinking. NLP, CBT and positive psychology all endeavour to change the structure of a person's thinking in order to create change.

Making changes at the level of structure is like playing with the shot selection, camera angles and soundtrack in a film. Running a film backwards can totally change its meaning. Playing funny music on the soundtrack can turn a tense, nail-biting scene into a humorous interlude. The world's finest film directors are masters at working with structure to create powerful experiences.

Level 4 – The nature of THOUGHT

THOUGHT creates our experience of reality; our experience of the world is created "from the inside-out." Insightfully understanding what's behind the scenes of our experience (seeing the *nature* of THOUGHT) can lead to a profound transformation, increasing clarity, security and peace of mind. People often experience a significant reduction in stress, and an increase in their sense of resiliency, regardless of external circumstances. Longstanding problems and issues often disappear without being "worked on."

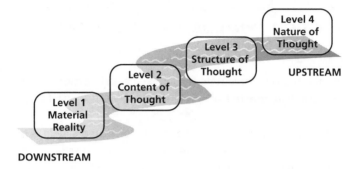

Figure 8.1 The Four Levels of Psychological Leverage

When it comes to films, the most powerful shift a person can experience is a shift in understanding. Once a person insightfully understands the nature of films, they can watch scenes which would previously have put them in fear for their lives.

Until a person understands the nature of films, it can really seem like that train is going to come out of the screen and get them.

But it won't. Ever. Because that's not the nature of films. It doesn't work that way.

Until a person understands the nature of movies, the best they can do is keep reminding themselves that "It's just a movie, it's just a movie…" Once a person insightfully understands the nature of movies, they don't have to do anything. No further intervention is necessary. They can still be deeply affected by a film, but they know that their well-being isn't at risk.

> *Until a person understands the nature of THOUGHT,*
> *intervention at the level of content or structure*
> *seems to make sense. Once you insightfully*
> *understand the nature of THOUGHT,*
> *intervention at the level of content*
> *or structure loses its appeal…*

The flying monkeys can't get out of the TV. The train's never getting out of the screen. Ever...

DISTINCTION: Externally-corrected vs. Self-correcting

A system that requires outside intervention in order to fix it can be referred to as **externally-corrected.** If a car breaks down, it won't fix itself. It needs an external agent to diagnose the problem, then take action to put it right. As the name suggests, a **self-correcting** system is one that corrects itself. It requires no external intervention. A self-correcting system merely requires the right conditions and enough time to resolve any issues. The primary condition needed for a self-correcting system to find its way back to balance is simple: an absence of external interference.

In Chapter 4, we drew the distinction between *applications* and *implications*. When you have even a basic understanding of the principles behind how some aspect of life always works (e.g. gravity, germs etc.), it has *implications* that are expressed in your thoughts, feelings and behaviours.

There are over 400 different psychological approaches or methodologies being used today in the worlds of business, personal development, coaching and therapy. Some of them are based on theories, others on heuristics or "rules of thumb." Almost every single one of them is an *application* model, relying on the change-worker to **externally-correct** the client's thinking (or the client to **externally-correct** their *own* thinking). The **external-correction** can take an infinite variety of forms; mental rehearsal, guided visualization, affirmations, techniques, psychoanalysis – they're all *applications*, and they're all working "downstream" from an understanding of the principle of THOUGHT. The worlds of business, personal development, coaching and therapy are awash with *application* models, attempts to **externally-correct** a **self-correcting** system.

Innate Thinking® is an *implication* model, focused on helping a client to insightfully understand the nature of THOUGHT, and the principles behind how our experience is created. With *Innate Thinking®*, there is no **external-correction**. Like understanding the nature of film, as soon as a person gets an insight into the nature of THOUGHT, their entire experience of reality starts to change. They start living in the *implications* of that understanding. *Innate Thinking*® facilitators and consultants work with clients to help them get an insight into the nature of THOUGHT, secure in the knowledge that the client really does have everything they need to **self-correct**; to find clarity, solve their problems, and create the results that matter to them.

If a child is frightened by the flying monkeys in *The Wizard of Oz*, you could use video-editing software to replace the monkeys with images of friendly kittens (a content change), or play funny music over the scene (a structure change). These changes would likely have some impact on their experience but, in the process, the child would be likely to accept and even reinforce the "reality" of the movie. "After all," the child would reason, "if it wasn't real, it wouldn't be necessary to make those changes, and they wouldn't have had such a big impact."

> *There's a huge difference between intervening in an existing "reality," versus looking upstream at what's creating that experiential reality.*

It's the same with application models. While they can definitely change a person's experience, they also run the risk of reinforcing the reality of the situation. Application models (by definition) deal with the products of THOUGHT, not the nature of THOUGHT. They are playing with what's already on the screen, while *Innate Thinking*® takes you behind the scenes, to how what's on the screen is being generated.

Remember: your perception of reality is less like looking out at the world through the lens of a camera, and more like wearing a pair of virtual reality goggles. What you're experiencing moment to moment is a THOUGHT-generated experiential reality. The "virtual reality goggles" of our perception are brought to life by the principles of innate thinking.

The power of understanding

I once collected my daughters from the home of a relative who was suffering from conjunctivitis (an extremely unpleasant and contagious infection of the eye membranes). I was careful not to touch anything, because I had a workshop to deliver, followed by a flight to California. The last thing I needed was a trip to the doctor.

The next day, I ate a hot, spicy meal, then sat down to watch a DVD with my children. That's when my eyes started itching. Over the course of the next 20 minutes, my eyes became more and more itchy, and my heart sank. I had conjunctivitis! My head filled with visions of doctors' waiting rooms, eye drops and cosmetic unpleasantness. When my misery reached epic proportions, I announced that I was going to take a shower.

The warm water had been running over my face and neck for about 90 seconds when a small, quiet voice inside me said *"You've got chilli sauce in your eyes."* In less than a second, my anxiety levels evaporated as my spirits rose like a hot-air balloon. The physical symptoms were just as unpleasant, but there was a key difference; I knew that the cause of my problem was a minor inconvenience (chilli sauce) not a serious problem (an eye infection).

In an instant, I popped from one experiential reality into another. As my head cleared, feelings of relief replaced the worry and frustration, and within a few minutes, my eyes were feeling better.

While this example is trivial, what it points to is essential. Most application models are attempting to deal with people's behaviours, and the feelings and thinking that generate them. But, in the process, they're accepting the illusionary reality implicit in that understanding of the world. Not only that, but they often give people *more* to think about, adding things on rather than taking things off their mind.

If a person doesn't understand that they're feeling their thinking in the moment, then they'll accept what their perception has to say about those feelings.

Thought creates the world then says "I didn't do it"...

On the other hand, the moment a person starts to insightfully understand the *nature* of THOUGHT, they experience a freedom in relation to the experiential reality it's generating. This represents a new paradigm for our understanding of the mind.

The power of a paradigm

The term "paradigm" was coined by Thomas Kuhn in his groundbreaking book, *The Structure of Scientific Revolutions* (listed by the *Times Literary Supplement* as one of "The Hundred Most Influential Books Since the Second World War"). *The Oxford English Dictionary* describes a paradigm (in the Kuhnian sense) as *"a worldview underlying the theories and methodology of a particular scientific subject."*

Kuhn explains that every scientific field has a pre-paradigm phase, during which the field has no shared basis or foundation to build upon. During this time, the field is beset by anomalies, with scientists working hard to explain them. Then, at a certain point, a paradigm emerges. Now the field has a shared foundation; a basis for further experiment and exploration. A new paradigm often results from the discovery of principles. For instance, Newton's discovery of the principle of gravity (and his resulting "law of universal gravitation") established a new paradigm for physics; a foundation on which subsequent work was based. Einstein's work on relativity established a further paradigm. Schrodinger's and Bohr's work on quantum physics established yet another, and so on.

The field of psychology has been in its pre-paradigm phase until now. This explains the plethora of (often conflicting) theories, techniques and models. It also explains the many thousands of books published each

---

year on personal development, business psychology and leadership models.

What the discovery of the principles underlying experience makes possible is *the realization of a single paradigm*; a worldview underlying the theories and methodology of all aspects of psychology.

When we shift from the pre-paradigm phase to the acceptance of a single paradigm, it has a profound impact. Consider the examples in the Table opposite.

Once a paradigm is established, it puts many pre-paradigm theories to rest. The flat-earth theory, the geo-centric universe and the miasma model are now seen as quaint historical curiosities. The principled, single-paradigm model of psychology (as summed up by the statement *"100% of our feeling is arising from* THOUGHT *in the moment"*) puts numerous other psychological models and theories to rest.

Superstitious thinking (the mistaken belief that we're feeling something *other than* THOUGHT in the moment) is bogus; a groundless illusion; as obsolete as the flat-earth theory, the geo-centric universe and the miasma model. Nevertheless, we all get deceived by this illusion on a regular basis.

The pioneering psychologist William James stated that if fundamental principles governing psychology were ever discovered, it would be the most important discovery for humanity since we mastered fire. The principles William James dreamt of have been discovered. Insightful understanding of this new paradigm is growing even as you read this book.

I've seen profound transformations in my clients as they get an understanding of the nature of THOUGHT. People start making progress on dreams that had seemed impossible until now. Business teams start working together and delivering results more creatively and effectively than ever before. Conflicts get resolved, and

Domain	Pre-paradigm	Post-paradigm
The solar system	Believed planet earth was the centre of universe. Calendars were inaccurate. Had to make occasional calendar adjustments to catch up. Difficulty predicting movement of planets etc.	Saw that the sun is the centre of the solar system. Calendars made more accurate. Greater ability to predict movement of planets etc.
Germ theory	Believed disease and illness was caused by a range of factors including miasmas and atmospheres. Doctors innocently made matters worse. Disease spread and exacerbated due to misunderstanding.	Near-universal awareness of germ theory. Individuals take sensible precautions to avoid illness. Doctors and nurses scrub up. Massive reduction in illness, and near-eradication of many diseases. Increased lifespan.
Flight	Countless attempts to create a manned, powered aircraft, using a variety of ingenious methods, with not a single successful flight.	The Wright brothers' discovery of the principles of aeronautics lead to manned aircraft, international jet travel, and the emergence of package holidays.

relationships get back on track. Clarity increases and performance improves. People suddenly discover that they've got more time in the day, as they spend less and less time in superstitious thinking. Individuals often start experiencing a quality of life and peace of mind unlike anything they've experienced until now.

And what's the source of the kind of clarity/creativity/presence/authenticity/motivation/connection/resilience/peace of mind and enjoyment of life most people yearn for?

I'll give you a hint: You've already got it...

keep exploring ⁘ connect with others
share your discoveries ⁘ deepen your understanding

Reflection point: *One of the more profound implications of the* Innate Thinking® *model is this: you don't need to control, monitor or manage your thinking. What happens when you stop for a moment and deeply consider that? For many people, this means a huge item is crossed off their metaphorical "to-do" list. You might even like to imagine some of the ways you can start enjoying all the extra time you've started freeing up...*

Have you heard the old saying that the best way to learn is to teach? While it's not always the case (there are many great ways to learn), there's a kernel of truth in it. When you share what you're learning with others within a short period of time, you create a whole new set of neural pathways, giving you a richer perspective on your discoveries. Scan the QR code with your smartphone or type the URL below into your browser. Once you've posted your comments, I invite you to explore the Chapter 8 resources, share them with your friends and explore some of the discoveries other people are posting about this chapter...

www.ClarityBook.biz/chapter8

PART TWO

The Deep Drivers

9

Innate Clarity and Peace of Mind

*"We don't know who discovered water,
but we know it wasn't the fish."*

Marshall McLuhan, Media theorist

"I don't need you to change. And I don't need anything from you. Whether you believe it or not, you don't need to do a thing..."

I burst into tears.

The year was 2004, and I'd just travelled several hundred miles to have a session with a coach. When I arrived, I explained that I really wanted to make some changes, and that I was totally committed to doing whatever I needed to do to get the most from our time together. I said that I felt like I really needed a breakthrough, and was worried that if I didn't "get it right," my time and money would be wasted, and I would be no further forward. Worse still, I would be stuck in the stress and dis-ease that had me come to him in the first place.

He told me I didn't need to do anything, and I burst into tears. And as I sat there with tears streaming down my face, I started to feel more peaceful.

We sat and talked for three hours, and by the time we were finished, I felt better than I had in ages. And I was so happy that I was feeling better, I didn't think to ask some obvious questions...

1 Where do the deep, rich, profound feelings in life come from?

2 Where do they go when you're not aware of them?

3 What are the factors determining whether you're aware of them or not?

Your understanding of how life works

Your understanding of how life works has more influence than any other factor over your experience of life, and the results you get. We each behave in accordance with what makes sense to us:

- In Aztec culture, it "made sense" to sacrifice people to the gods in order to keep the community thriving.

- In England in the 1850s, it "made sense" to dump raw sewage into the River Thames and carry small bunches of flowers to protect against illness.

- In Japanese culture, it "makes sense" for many people to work 12 hours a day, 6 days a week, for months or even years on end, with an inevitable toll on their health (the Japanese even have a word, *karōshi*, which means literally "death from overwork").

In 2004, my understanding of "how life works" dictated that all feelings and states could be recreated, accessed and utilized by manipulating a person's body, their breathing, and their thought patterns.

Mental-emotional states were something a person "chose," "got into," and "managed." I endeavoured to direct, alter and manage my thought patterns in order to experience the states, feelings and emotions I wanted.

I saw states, feelings and emotions as a "result." They were something I "did." If I wasn't feeling the way I wanted to feel, it just meant that I wasn't choosing, getting into or managing the states well enough.

In the cultures of NLP, CBT and positive psychology, it "makes sense" to focus on directing, managing and controlling your thinking in order to experience the states you believe will serve you.

But, as you start to understand innate thinking more clearly, the idea of *controlling* your states shows a misunderstanding of what states, feelings and emotions are. Once you start to get an insightful understanding of the single paradigm, the idea of "state control" stops making sense.

You have innate clarity and peace of mind

Clarity and peace of mind are the "default position" for people – the factory settings. While these are context-sensitive – they can show up differently depending on the situation – they're the baseline for a person when there's nothing else in the way. And what gets in the way? Superstitious thinking.

Like a football being held underwater, as soon as you let go, it rises to the surface. And like the grass pressing up through the cracks in a city pavement, your resilience and clarity is always doing its best to find its way through the paving slabs of your superstitious thinking.

If you have any doubt about this, consider little children. Up to the age of around four years old, children return easily to the default setting of their clarity and well-being. While they often get upset, they don't stay with it. The pull of their clarity is too strong, and their superstitious thinking is not powerful enough to keep them from it.

Clarity is the small child's standard setting. Think about it. The average three-year-old:

- Tends to be deeply engaged, easily amused and satisfied with the simple joys of life; is present and in the moment.

- Doesn't know the meaning of the word "bored"; can enjoy the same things over and over again.

- Is loving and open-hearted, connecting easily with others.

- Finds lots of things fun and funny.

- Comes up with new ideas and creative insights.

- Knows they don't really understand how life works; is curious, often puzzled, and constantly learning.

- Gets over upsets quickly and easily; doesn't tend to dwell on past mistakes or worry about the future.

- Is in touch with their deeper wisdom, often aware of "the elusive obvious" that the adults around them aren't seeing.

The average three-year-old spends a lot of their time in clarity, because they're allowing their psychology to do what it's designed to do. Ironically, the extremes of emotion that little children swing back and forth between would look *certifiable* on the average adult, but that's because children aren't trying to manage their states. The psychology of little children is an example of the mind's self-correcting system given the freedom to do what it does best; return to a set-point of clarity and well-being.

Think of a child's gyroscope. When the gyroscope spins, it naturally gravitates towards a vertical alignment. If you knock it off centre, it self-corrects, and makes its way back towards the vertical. You don't need to do anything to correct it – in fact, efforts to correct it tend to *impede* its progress.

> *The mind is a self-correcting system. Its set-point*
> *is clarity, resilience and well-being...*

Case Study: *Dragon's Den*

Rich Enion was in a bind. He had just appeared on TV's *Dragon's Den* seeking funding for *BassToneSlap*, a business providing drumming-based performances, team-building and experiential marketing events. Dragons Peter Jones and Theo Paphitis had just offered him and his business partner £50,000 for a 40% share in the company. The offer had sounded good on the programme, but when it came time to sign contracts, he was having second thoughts. While Rich was tempted by the prospect of a healthy cash injection, the thought of surrendering a big chunk of his business and profits was daunting. He was stuck in a dilemma and didn't know what to do.

Rich asked my advice, so I talked to him about the nature of THOUGHT, the reality principle. I explained that his feelings of doubt and confusion weren't coming from the deal, the money, the percentages or the potential results; they were coming from his thinking. As we continued exploring, Rich got quiet. After a few moments of silent reflection, he took a deep breath and said he had the answer. I asked him what had occurred to him, and he said *"Freedom!"*

Rich explained that the appearance on *Dragon's Den* had been the result of an authentic desire, and many months of hard work and focus. He'd intuitively known what an incredible opportunity it was. The offer of investment seemed like the icing on the cake but, somewhere along the way, Rich had lost sight of why he and his partner created *BassToneSlap* in the first place... Freedom! From Rich's perspective, the purpose of the business was so they could create great experiences for clients while doing something they loved, with plenty of space in the diary for travel and adventure.

When Rich got clear and re-connected with the purpose for the business, he realized that signing the contract with the Dragons would be a wrong turn. They declined the £50,000, and stayed connected with the vision. *BassToneSlap* has grown into a very successful business; Rich has a number of teams that he joins for performances when he's in the UK. The rest of the time, he runs his business from exotic locations around the world, enjoying the freedom he's found.

The benefits of allowing the mind to find its *own* way back to clarity vastly outweigh the benefits of external intervention. Why? Because external intervention stops the self-correcting system doing its job.

Clarity is what a person's psychology is always endeavouring to return to. Innate clarity and resilience are always shining a beacon, even when a person seems hopelessly lost...

Modello, Homestead Gardens and Coliseum Gardens

In the mid-1980s, Dr Roger Mills introduced "Health Realization" (a community-oriented presentation of the inside-out understanding) to residents of Modello and Homestead Gardens; two Florida housing projects that had become havens for drug dealers, and hotbeds of addiction, crime and abuse.

At first, the residents were suspicious of this man trying to point them towards the clarity and well-being he said was already within them. They (understandably) saw their horrific circumstances and backgrounds as the source of their problems. But slowly, people began to catch on, and get a feel for the direction Dr Mills was pointing them in.

By the time the programme completed two years later, the community had seen a greater than 50 percent improvement in employment levels, school attendance and parent/school involvement. The drug-dealers had gone, and there was a massive decrease in criminal activity.

Residents had found their innate clarity and peace of mind.

The experiment was repeated in Oakland's Coliseum and Lockwood Gardens. The homicide rate in these housing projects went from being the highest in the city to zero – a level they remained at for the next ten years. In addition to the zero homicide rate, violent crimes dropped by 45 percent. Police officer Jerry Williams received the California Peace Prize in 1997 for his leadership of the initiative.

Innate clarity, well-being and resilience exist within every person; it's your natural state, a fact you become particularly aware of when you've got nothing on your mind. In fact, there's nothing you need to "do" to have an awareness of your innate clarity and peace of mind; it's more of a "not-doing." You see...

*Clarity isn't an achievement;
it's a pre-existing condition...*

It's not something you need to practice or "work on." It's an expression of who you really are.

MIND, the power principle, shows up in every aspect of our experience, gently pointing us towards clarity and well-being. Clarity is there within each one of us, tirelessly working to guide us in the direction of our most inspiring, rewarding and meaningfully successful lives.

When you turn your attention away from the grinding familiarity of habitual thinking, you make space for clarity, and the powerful inevitability of fresh, new thought. That's when you find yourself looking in the most generative, nourishing and resourceful direction there is…

---

keep exploring ❖ connect with others
share your discoveries ❖ deepen your understanding

Reflection point: What happens when you open to the possibility that clarity and peace of mind are your "default settings"?

Clarity and peace of mind are the set-point your psychology is always endeavouring to guide you back to. From this perspective, we can see the "logic" behind seemingly unhealthy behaviours. The realization that you're always in the process of restoring yourself to the "default settings" can be remarkably freeing. Whenever you're ready, type the URL below into your browser or scan the QR code with your smartphone. There can be huge value in sharing your insights and a-has with other people who are on a journey similar to your own…

www.ClarityBook.biz/chapter9

10

Creativity and Disruptive Innovation

"You don't learn to walk by following rules. You learn by doing, and by falling over."

Richard Branson, Entrepreneur,
founder of Virgin Group

"It just occurred to me when I was out for a walk in the woods..."

In 2003, I started a business creating educational products. My main marketing tool was an email list. Each week, I wrote an article and sent it to my subscribers. By the end of the first year, 5000 people had subscribed to my articles, when I had a sudden insight. Google had recently launched "Adwords," the little adverts that show up when you search the web. I could run ads for my newsletter and pay a low price for each new subscriber. It was years before anyone else caught on.

By 2008, I had one of the largest email lists in the industry, with over 80,000 subscribers in my "tribe." I explained my adword "secret" to a marketing expert who was interviewing me, and he asked me where I got the idea. *"I don't know,"* I said, *"It just occurred to me when I was out for a walk in the woods."*

Now I know where that innovative new idea came from; it came from the unknown...

DISTINCTION: The known vs. The unknown

- **The known** is the database of thoughts you've already thought, including your habitual ways of thinking about yourself, your life and your world. By definition, the thoughts you've already had are rooted in the past; while they can hold valuable information, they're "yesterday's news" and can only tell you about what was.

- **The unknown** is the source of all fresh, new thoughts; the formless power of THOUGHT. When we have clarity, our minds are free from superstitious thinking, and we create space for new thinking to flow in. (All your **"known"** thoughts originally came from the **unknown** too, back when they were fresh, new and relevant.)

When people are looking for solutions, they tend to look to what they already know, but all too often the answers we need can't be found there. When we want fresh new ideas, creativity, solutions and changes, it pays to look in the direction of **the unknown.**

---

*Looking to the database of the known for navigating the future
is like looking in the rear-view mirror to find your way forward...*

Disruptive innovation

The pace of change is accelerating and our world is getting more complex. "Disruptive innovation" is the watchword, as whipper-snapper start-ups steal market share from major players, or even take the market in a new direction. One of the surprising things about this is how often the major players peer into the database of the known, stuck in "analysis paralysis" as a new entrant gobbles up their market.

The music industry was like a rabbit in the headlights in 1999 when Napster enabled millions of users to share their music collections with each other. The record companies responded by suing Napster and threatening their own customers, but didn't come up with a credible alternative. Instead, they tried to hang on to a model designed for a world that no longer existed. They looked to the database of the known for the answer, and came up empty-handed; their revenues dropped by 50% in between 2001 and 2010. Meanwhile, Apple's visionary leader Steve Jobs was watching this drama unfold. Apple launched the iTunes store in 2003, making it possible for customers to purchase and download music online *legally*. Apple threw a life preserver to the music business, and gave their customers what they *really* wanted, becoming the world's most profitable company in the process.

Case Study: Failing forward towards success

Back in the 1990s, the publishing industry was heading into a crisis. The twin challenges of desktop publishing and the internet were threatening the industry's lucrative role as "middleman" between content creators (authors) and content consumers (readers).

At the time, I was working as a consultant, running organizational change programmes for a large publishing group with a number of businesses under its umbrella. Two of the companies provided a sharp contrast:

Company A was a well-established firm, centuries old, with a reputation for accuracy, consistency and reliability.

Company B was a relatively new start-up that had carved out a decent market share using a combination of technology and process innovation.

As the crisis became more acute, the two businesses behaved in very different ways:

Company A responded by organizing committees and working groups to assess the situation and propose strategic responses. The committees and working groups met, researched and ruminated. Years passed as they sought out "the perfect strategy."

Company B had a completely different response. They immediately started developing innovative new products and launching them. Many of these products failed, but some of them didn't. The company built on the successes and incorporated the lessons into the next tranche of products. The combination of fresh new thinking and real world feedback proved to be a winning formula.

When I asked the managing director of **Company B** what his secret was, he said "It's simple: You fail forward towards success."

While **Company A** was treading water, searching fruitlessly in their database of old thinking, **Company B** was enjoying rapid growth and product innovation by looking to what they didn't yet know; coming up with fresh ideas, taking action and learning from their results.

This situation proceeded until the early 2000s when, in an unexpected reversal of fortune, **Company B** was overtaken by more innovative competitors. **Company A**, on the other hand, brought in a consultant and the CEO from **Company B**. They proceeded to build a product innovation capacity outside their normal operations, before importing it (and its innovation culture) back into the core business. Since then, **Company A** has performed well, out-innovating its competitors with an effective mix of fresh thinking, action and feedback.

The gap

Epistemologist Gregory Bateson said that problems result from the difference between how nature works and the way people think. If we try to navigate using an out-of-date map, we run into problems; our thinking is out of step with how the world is working. But the music industry (and many other businesses) clung to the map of their habitual thinking in the face of overwhelming evidence that it was no longer fit for purpose. Why?

Lack of clarity.

The only explanation for this bizarre behaviour is that they were lost in superstitious thinking, hypnotized by the outside-in misunderstanding, unable to see clearly. Superstitious thinking can make it look as though the unknown is dangerous, and the database of habitual thinking is a safe refuge, but nothing could be further from the truth. Grinding away at habitual thinking is like chewing an old piece of gum – it never gives you what you want.

So what's the alternative? Insightful understanding.

Insightful understanding closes the gap
between how life works and how you think…

What showers and vacations have in common

Senior executives in the USA were surveyed and asked where and when they tended to get their best ideas. The top three answers were as follows:

1. *On vacation*

2. *In the shower*

3. *While travelling to and from the office*

The ideas that really made a difference to these business people arrived at the very times that they *weren't* thinking about work; in situations where they weren't looking for answers in what they already knew.

Almost everyone can relate to this and find their own examples of fresh, new thought arriving when the mind is in a more relaxed, contemplative state. Yet, all too often, when people want to find an answer, solution or fresh new idea, they start grinding away at what they already know; running through their habitual thinking patterns one more time.

Ironically, the habitual thinking they're grinding away at is typically the only thing standing between a person and a fresh new idea. Superstitious thinking is "the box" that corporate facilitators are habitually telling us we need to "think outside" of.

Throughout history, many of the most profound and groundbreaking new ideas did not come from manipulations of what people already knew; they came from the unknown, in the form of insights and sudden "a-ha" moments:

- The Greek mathematician, physicist and inventor Archimedes had been grappling with the problem of how to determine the volume of a golden crown which King Hiero II suspected of being impure. One day, as he climbed into his bath, Archimedes saw the water level rise, and had a sudden realization about how he could solve the problem. He shouted "Eureka" and ran naked into the street. He'd been working fruitlessly within what he already knew as he'd tried to "figure out" the problem, but his insight came from a new thought; from a fresh new perspective. It came from the unknown.

- By 1666, Isaac Newton had already been struggling for some time to describe the workings of gravity. One day, sitting in his mother's garden in "a contemplative mood," he happened to see an apple fall from a tree. Suddenly, he had an insight about the nature of gravity. Newton's theory of gravitation grew from this fresh, new thought; a thought that came from beyond what he already knew, from the unknown.

- In 1920, Otto Loewi (the father of neuroscience) was fast asleep when he had a dream in which he envisaged an experiment that could prove conclusively how nerve impulses were transmitted. Scientists had been theorizing about it for 15 years, but Loewi's new thought took the field from theory to fact. Loewi's fresh idea came from the unknown.

Of course, the unknown isn't just available to scientists and mathematicians. We all have a source of fresh new thinking, beyond what we already know...

- The insight that gives you the elegant solution for something which had you stumped.

- The realization that has you understand something which used to baffle you.

- The "a-ha moment" that gives you a fresh new perspective on a situation.

- The clear mind that allows you to remember where you left something you'd been frantically searching for.

Whether you call it an insight, a realization, or an "a-ha" moment, new arrivals from the unknown almost always come with a feeling of peace and clarity, a gentle rightness and "knowing" that feels fresh and new.

So if the unknown is such a rich and powerful resource, why are so many people "afraid of the unknown," building elaborate structures of stale, superstitious thinking as a vain attempt to protect them against what they don't yet know?

Every vertebrate intuitively knows that, in the material world, the unknown can be an unpredictable place of potential risks and rewards, while the known may have a proven track record of safety, security and predictability.

But we make a mistake when we attribute the same qualities to the world of our thinking.

The known of our thinking is often like an out-of-date map that doesn't show any recent developments; the new streets, parks and paths of possibility. We can search the map as much as we like, but we won't find something wonderful that's just around the corner (or right there in front of us) if the map doesn't mention it.

So, if it's off the map, where can you find it? And how can you benefit from the clarity, resilience and peace of mind that it brings?

---

keep exploring ❖ connect with others
share your discoveries ❖ deepen your understanding

Reflection point: Has it ever occurred to you that anywhere you've been feeling stuck until now is an example of thinking that's become stale and rigid? But like a loaf of bread, warm from the baker's oven, all that stale thinking was once fresh, new and current. And just like there's no way to "un-stale" a loaf of bread, there's no way to freshen thinking that's past its use-by date. Fortunately, that doesn't matter. The principles of innate thinking are like the baker's oven. They're always ready to produce fresh, new thinking as soon as it occurs to you that you won't find the answer in what you already know.

Once you've finished reflecting on this for now, scan the QR code or pop over to the website to post your comments and keep exploring. If you come across something you'd like to share with your friends and colleagues, feel free! While you're at it, you can get a peek at what other people are saying...

www.ClarityBook.biz/chapter10

11

Authenticity: Your True Identity

....

*"Matter flows from place to place
and momentarily comes together to be you.
Whatever you are, therefore, you are not
the stuff of which you are made."*

Richard Dawkins, Evolutionary biologist

"You are not your job. You are not how much money you have in the bank..."

These two "un-firmations" echo through the 1999 film *Fight Club* like an incantation. Fincher's classic film (and the Chuck Palahniuk book it is based on) raises questions about meaning, identity, and the consumerist dream. In the process, it strips away the false identities of many of the characters, through a mixture of fighting, fellowship and harrowing ordeals. And, while the film continues to detail "who you aren't" (you are not the shoes that you wear, the contents of your wallet etc.), it's less specific about who you *are*...

A case of mistaken identity

Stop for a moment and touch your nose. Say the words "This is my nose."

I've invited countless members of my audiences, training groups and corporate teambuilding sessions to perform this simple task over the years. Everyone finds it easy to do, yet few of us consider the extraordinary accomplishments that make this possible.

When you were born, you didn't realize that you had a nose, eyes and a face. Your hands and fingers were mysterious objects that emitted sensations and occasionally bumped into your head. You had no sense of them being "yours," or of being able to control them.

But then something amazing happened...

You started to make a map; a map of *you*. It started with your body, your immediate environment and your parents. The map of your body let you define the relationships between different parts of your body – essential for being able to perform actions like touching your nose or grasping an object.

You also created a map of "who you are"; a map which you've been updating ever since. This map of "who you are" is sometimes called the self-image, self-concept or ego.

The self-image gets used as a reference point for living, giving you an opinion on what you're capable of, where your limits are, what you deserve, what's important etc. Whether you think something's possible for you or not, it's likely that you automatically check with your self-image to find out its opinion, one way or another.

But here's the thing: your self-image is just a THOUGHT-generated map/model. It's not who you really are.

And while none of us would ever make the mistake of confusing a map of New York City with the city itself, we all make this same mistake when we confuse our self-image with who we really are.

You see, just as a *map* of New York is not New York, your *ideas* about you are not you. We each fall into the trap of thinking our ideas about ourselves describe the entirety of who we are, but it's a case of mistaken identity.

You are not your ideas about yourself.
You are not the contents or structure of your thinking.
And who you really are is far, far more than you think you are...

Not only are you not your job, your bank balance or the shoes you wear...

- you are not your body
- you are not your accomplishments
- you are not your history
- you are not your prospects
- you are not your ideas about yourself
- you are not your theories about what is or isn't possible for you
- you are not your self-image, self-concept or ego
- in fact, you aren't the contents or structure of your thinking at all.

Think about it: If "who you really are" was your body, your self-image, or how you feel about yourself, then these things would never change; they would be constant. But that's not the case:

- **Your body.** Your body changes as you grow, age and develop. If you look at a picture of yourself from ten years ago, there are almost certainly differences. Our bodies are made mostly from water, and all the cells are frequently replaced. In fact, most of the cells in your body are less than ten years old! Who a person truly is doesn't change, but their body does. You call it "my body," but who is the "me" whose body it is?

- **Your self-image.** How you think about yourself changes as you learn and grow, and as you go in and out of superstitious thinking. One day a person comes home from work feeling bad about themselves. The next day they wake up feeling great about themselves. Who you really are doesn't change, but how you *perceive* yourself does. You call your thinking "my thinking," but who is the one who's having an experience of your thinking?

- **Your feelings.** Your feelings change on a daily basis; you're living in the feeling of your thinking. You call your feelings "my feelings," but who is the one who's feeling them? You refer to yourself as "me," but who is the one who is having an experience of being you?

Even trying to answer these questions can take you into a curious state, because they point in the direction of what I'm calling the formless. So, if all of this is who you *aren't*, who *are* you?

Who you *really* are is what's *creating* your experience; the intelligent, formless energy behind life; the principles of innate thinking: THOUGHT, CONSCIOUSNESS and MIND.

It's odd to think of who we really are as "energy," but it also stands to reason. Science tells us that everything is made of energy, that the atoms that make up our bodies are mostly space. The law of conservation of energy (a principle of the first law of thermodynamics) states:

Energy can be neither created nor destroyed.
However, energy can change forms,
and energy can flow from one place to another.

Richard Dawkins says that we are more like waves than things. He explains that all the atoms that were in our bodies as children have been replaced; that whatever we *may* be, we're not the "stuff" of our physical bodies. Different cultures and traditions through the ages have had a variety of ways of describing what we are and where we come from:

- consciousness

- soul

- big mind

- spirit

- natural intelligence

- divine energy

- God.

Each of these words are metaphors, pointing to something formless, intangible and constant; a "true identity" that sits behind the fleeting but tangible illusion of our material reality.

So how is this relevant?

The spiritual dimension and performance

In their January 2001 *Harvard Business Review* article, "The Making of a Corporate Athlete," Jim Loehr and Tony Schwartz explain that, in addition to their physical, mental and emotional capacity, the most successful senior executives and entrepreneurs also attend to their "spiritual capacity," which they define as follows:

"By spiritual capacity, we simply mean the energy that is unleashed by tapping into one's deepest values and defining a strong sense of purpose. This capacity, we have found, serves as sustenance in the face of adversity and as a powerful source of motivation, focus, determination, and resilience."

As you'll appreciate, the terms "deepest values" and "sense of purpose" are simply metaphors; forms that point to something deeper. Words like "team spirit" and "inspiration" are other examples of an attempt to point to something that comes before our world of form.

Who you really are is the formless energy behind life; the principles of innate thinking. These principles are also the source of your security, well-being, peace, joy and happiness, which means...

You already are *what you've been searching for until now...*

There's nothing to search for – you've already got it; you already *are* it. There's nowhere to get to – you're already here... You don't need improving, fixing or developing – who you already are is the all-encompassing energy behind life!

Stop for a moment and consider the planet we live on. As you're reading these words, the energy behind life is moving from form-less into form, and back again:

- babies are being born
- flowers are blooming
- forest fires are burning
- birds are flying
- nearly seven billion people are breathing in and out (including everyone you know)
- leaves are falling to the ground and fallen branches are disintegrating

- the hearts of every living mammal on the planet are beating
- creatures are dying
- water is evaporating
- sub-atomic particles are moving in and out of existence
- countless billions of thoughts are emerging then disappearing
- rain is falling
- and on, and on, and on... all of this as you're reading these words...

Behind all of this is the energy behind life. It shows up in all the processes of your body and all the workings of your mind.

It is what's creating your experience of reality, and it is what's perceiving the experience of the reality it's creating.

To paraphrase Cobb (the lead character from *Inception*) once again...

> "*In your waking experience of reality, innate thinking continuously creates and perceives a world simultaneously... So completely that it doesn't even feel itself doing the creating.*"

So, if who we really are is this extraordinary intelligence, the formless energy behind life, why do we so often look, feel and act as though we're neither intelligent nor extraordinary? You guessed it; superstitious thinking, and the outside-in misunderstanding that gives rise to it.

It's entirely natural and understandable that we get fooled by our thinking. But we can also wake up to a greater clarity of understanding, and to our innate security, resilience and peace of mind in any moment.

The War of the Worlds

On Halloween night, 1938, Orson Welles directed the radio version of H G Wells' novel, *The War of the Worlds*. It was a radio play with a difference; Welles presented it in the form of a news broadcast, giving a "live report" of New Jersey being invaded by Martians. He made it as realistic as possible, even getting the actors to study newsreels of the Hindenburg disaster so they could replicate the panic and terror in the voices of the announcers.

As far as numerous listeners were concerned, they had tuned in to a live news report. They reacted with shock and terror as they heard descriptions of tentacled Martians using heat-rays to incinerate their fellow Americans. There was widespread panic, and some people even armed themselves and took to the streets.

They were responding to a THOUGHT-generated illusion as though it was a material reality.

The police were swamped with calls from terrified listeners. They told them all the same thing:

"It's just a radio show."

While a few callers may not have believed the police at first, we can imagine how most of them responded…

Waves of relief…

Relief, peace and even laughter are natural responses, the moment you realize you've been responding to a mind-made illusion, not a material reality. The moment they saw that it was a radio show and not a news report, their "problem" was solved.

And how much effort did it take them to see the truth? None.

We can each wake up to a greater clarity of understanding in any moment. No matter how deeply asleep we are, we're only ever one thought away from waking up. No matter how lost you sometimes get in thoughts of lack, worry and insecurity, who you really are is always the same…

Peace, freedom, wisdom, clarity and love. *You* are what you've been searching for. Resilience, creativity, security, confidence and joy. You already *are* the source of all you desire; the energy behind life.

And just as a wave is not separate from the ocean,
who you really are is not separate
from the energy of the universe…

By the way, I don't mean energy in a "woo-woo," New Age sense. I mean it in a more down-to-earth, scientific, *"this is the logical extension of what leading physicists are telling us,"* sense.

So how can you align yourself with how the world already works? Fortunately, you've been provided with an elegant, accurate and reliable tool for navigating life, deepening your understanding, guiding you back to clarity and having a richer experience than you may have ever thought possible…

keep exploring ⁙ connect with others
share your discoveries ⁙ deepen your understanding

Reflection point: What happens when you consider the fact that clarity, peace and security are only ever one thought away? A change in thinking is the most natural thing in the world. The moment it occurs to you that you are feeling your thinking, and nothing else, you know the process of self-correction has begun.

Isn't it nice to know that this incredible power is "pre-loaded" into who you really are; an aspect of your true nature? If you feel like it, head over to the URL below or scan the QR code to keep exploring and sharing what you're discovering. After all, there's always more...

www.ClarityBook.biz/chapter11

12

Intuition: Navigating by Wisdom

"Don't let the noise of others' opinions drown out your own inner voice. And, most important, have the courage to follow your heart and intuition. They somehow already know what you truly want to become. Everything else is secondary."

Steve Jobs, Entrepreneur,
co-founder of Apple

(Stanford Commencement Speech, 2005[1])

---

1   'You've got to find what you love, Jobs says', *Stanford Report*, 14 June 2005   http://news.stanford.edu/news/2005/june15/jobs-061505.html

"All that the pathfinder needs is his senses and knowledge of how to interpret nature's signs..."

In his book *Nature Is Your Guide: How to Find Your Way on Land and Sea*, record-breaking navigator Harold Gatty claims that there is no such thing as a sense of direction. He explains that a person who appears to have such a "sense" is actually using their five ordinary senses (**seeing, hearing, smelling, tasting and feeling**), informing and informed by their experience and intelligence.

Gatty was a pioneer in the early years of aviation navigation. Before the existence of autopilot and other modern navigation technologies, Gatty mastered the art of using minimal cues from the natural world to orient the crafts he guided around the world; setting a direction, making adjustments and staying on-track.

Today we have GPS satellite navigation and numerous other technologies, yet we still rely on our senses for much of our day-to-day orientation. Whether we're walking down a city street, moving around our living space or driving to a friend's house, we're supported in our journeys by our five senses, our intelligence and our experience.

But we make a mistake when we try to use exactly the same "navigation system" to make our way through life. Consider these statements:

- "I want to get clarity on my overall life-path before I take the next step."

- "I'm stuck. My life's at a roadblock and I need to get moving."

- "I need to define my values and purpose so I can start heading in the right direction."

Remember: people tend to think, speak and act as though their thought-forms have the same qualities as the material world.

We use material-world metaphors for our work; for our lives; for our problems. We bring those metaphors to life using innate thinking, then respond to them as though they're a material reality. We say that life's a journey, a struggle, or an adventure, then start behaving as though that's actually the case!

When it comes to making our way through life, it seems as though the "navigation systems" that work in the material world should also work in the world of our life-metaphors. For example: if life's a journey, then it stands to reason that you need to get clear on the destination, find a good map and ensure you take the right steps. If life's a game, then it looks as though you need to find out how to play, learn what the rules are, and most importantly, that you win. If life's a battle, then it makes sense to focus on weapons, strategy and tactics.

But life is not a journey, a game or a battle. Life isn't a bed of roses, a bowl of cherries or a box of chocolates. Life isn't a struggle, a lesson or even an adventure...

Life just is.

So if life "just is," how can we live a life we love? If we go beyond the comforting familiarity of our material-world metaphors, how do we know where to go, what to do, or what we even want?

The bad news is that metaphors are inherent in our language; any verbal answer to the above questions will be strewn with them. The good news is that it doesn't matter. You see...

> *You have a built-in guidance system;*
> *it's called wisdom...*

Wisdom is an expression of MIND: the power principle. As such, it comes from *before* the world of form, from outside of our perceptual domain of time, space and matter. While intellect and past experience can be a valuable source of data, wisdom provides a different calibre of information. It's a context-sensitive, up-to-the-minute guidance system that comes from *before* your habitual thinking, from the intelligent energy behind life.

As the information on the DVD exists prior to (and gives rise to) the forms on the TV screen, so wisdom exists prior to our THOUGHT-generated experiential reality.

Sat-nav for your life

Your habitual, superstitious thinking is like an out-of-date map, a distorted snapshot of the world taken at the time it was created. It may have its uses, but the fact that you've already thought it means it's out of date. Wisdom, on the other hand, is like a constantly updated "super sat-nav" system for your life. Wisdom comes from *before* your habitual thinking, so it's never out of date.

Even a map you made as recently as last week can't possibly respond to road closures and traffic jams, but a high-quality sat-nav can.

And where is the sat-nav of your wisdom navigating you to? It's helping you find your way back home to who you really are, so you can have a richer, deeper, more fulfilling experience of life... so you can enjoy the high performance and good decisions that come from a clear mind... so you can create what you're inspired to create... so you can benefit from the innovation, resilience and clarity you need to prosper in times of uncertainty, complexity and change.

This innate wisdom is distinct from intellect and experience, so it's not dependent on any of the factors that are often cited as being associated with wisdom. It's unconnected with education, background, intellect, age and experience (little children, for example, sometimes exhibit a deep wisdom and intelligence about life despite their early years).

Why?

Because all of these "factors" are based in the world of form. But wisdom is an emanation from *before* the form; wisdom comes direct from the formless energy behind life. Everybody has the wisdom of the universe within them. No one has access to more wisdom than anyone else.

Who's on your "Top 3 Wisest People Ever" List?

- Buddha, Christ and Muhammad?

- Socrates, Plato and Aristotle?

- Queen Elizabeth I, Abraham Lincoln, Margaret Thatcher?

- Galileo, Isaac Newton and Marie Curie?

- Anne Frank, Ayn Rand, John Lennon?

- Albert Einstein, Stephen Hawking, Jane Goodall?

- Mohandas Gandhi, Rosa Parks, Nelson Mandela?

- Richard Branson, Anita Roddick, Steve Jobs?

Whoever's on your list, none of them has/had more wisdom within them than you. You have the same wisdom within you as the wisest people in history. So, how do you become more and more open to wisdom, and allow it to guide you?

It's already guiding you, moment to moment...

In *Nature Is Your Guide*, Gatty makes the point that we use our sense organs instinctively. We don't have to be taught to use them; you didn't have to go to classes on how to see, hear, feel, taste or smell. The ability to use the senses arrives bundled with the senses themselves. Your ability to use your senses is innate. Some people are more attuned to certain senses than others, but we're all expressing an innate ability.

It's the same with wisdom...

- When you're feeling more and more agitated as you think about something someone did last week... that's wisdom, activating "psychological pain-withdrawal reflex."

- When you're lost in superstitious thinking, and it suddenly occurs to you that you're feeling your thoughts... that's wisdom, pointing you back in the right direction.

- When you finally stop ruminating on a problem and the answer suddenly arrives... that's wisdom, penetrating the veneer of habitual thinking.

- When you're soaking in the tub and a flash of insight lets you know exactly how to proceed in an area where you were blocked... that's wisdom, giving you strategic guidance (in fact, the wisdom that gives you a brainwave often arrives when you're doing something else).

- The wisdom that comes with clarity is typically accompanied by a good feeling; a sense of peaceful knowing that's very distinct from the "fervent rightness" of our habitual thinking.

- Bear in mind that wisdom is looking out for your best interests. That doesn't mean that everyone's going to *like* what you do when you act on your wisdom, but they'll often be able to "see the wisdom" in it.

- Wisdom often seems obvious in retrospect; people say things like "I don't understand how I didn't see it before."

- Wisdom is the source of insight, and you've already been acting on it in a variety of ways throughout your life.

Strategic intuition

William Duggan is a senior lecturer in business management on Columbia University's MBA courses. In his award-winning book, *Strategic Intuition*, he explains that the flashes of insight that are so often the source of brilliant strategy almost *never* happen when people are thinking about the matter at hand.

Instead, they come when we're in the shower, or driving, or on holiday; when we're present to a more reflective state, allowing our minds to wander.

So, if the solution to our most pressing problems is to be found in reflection and relaxation, why are we so tempted to chew away at them like a dog with a bone?

Superstitious thinking.

When we're caught up in the misunderstanding, the feelings that accompany what we're thinking about can make it feel like grinding away at it is a good idea; but that's a misinterpretation of a valid signal (see Chapter 5).

Isn't it nice to know that, even when you haven't been aware of it, you've been guided by wisdom your whole life? It's good to see wisdom as the ordinary, everyday thing that it is. As you allow yourself to become more and more attuned to your wisdom, you may be surprised at just how easily you notice and are guided by it in your life.

Of course, as your understanding of innate thinking deepens, and you're guided more and more by your wisdom, it's inevitable that your experience of life will get better and better (though you're guaranteed to have ups and downs along the way). And, while people often find themselves getting better results at work and in all areas of their lives, you may also find that some of the things which *used* to seem important to you, no longer are.

From coaches to soap-makers

Two of my clients, a couple, started working with me to help get their coaching business on-track alongside their day jobs. As they got a deeper understanding of the principles behind innate thinking, they experienced an "inner relaxation," and made a startling discovery; they were both passionate about making organic soap! They started researching and experimenting, with a sense of joy and ease that was as refreshing as the soap samples they started sharing with their friends. They'd been struggling to make progress on the coaching business, but their passion for the soap business made it easy to do what had to be done. They're now on the verge of moving to the South of France to officially launch their new venture.

As you allow yourself to be guided by wisdom, you create space for a deeper pattern of life to emerge. As you start living from a deeper understanding of innate thinking, the circumstances of your life move into alignment with your deeper understanding.

So, does that mean that the circumstances of your life are all going to be a bed of roses? Not necessarily. Everyone has hardships to go through and losses to deal with. Furthermore, you don't know if your idea of what a great life looks like *today* will even appeal to you as you live life with a greater clarity of understanding.

So, if we're being guided by wisdom, where does that leave the whole domain of goal-setting?

I've got some good news and some bad news for you...

**keep exploring ⁙ connect with others
share your discoveries ⁙ deepen your understanding**

Reflection point: How good does it feel to realize that you have an incredibly reliable inner guidance system? A means of navigation that's always helping you out with clear, context-sensitive, up-to-the-minute information...

It can come as a bit of a shock to realize you've had this valuable tool with you for your whole life, even when you weren't aware of it. And, as you continue becoming increasingly aware of your wisdom and intuition, you'll find yourself relying on it more and more. You might even like to compare notes with others about some of the ways you've already begun to notice your wisdom showing up for you. Just scan the QR code below, or enter the URL into your browser to keep sharing what you're learning and explore even more resources for deepening your understanding...

www.ClarityBook.biz/chapter12

13

Toxic Goals and Authentic Desires

"All great things are done for their own sake."

Robert Frost, Poet, playwright

"Escape 9–5, live anywhere, and join the new rich..."

I read Tim Ferriss' lifestyle-hacking manifesto, *The 4-Hour Work Week* upon its release in 2007, and I was electrified! I'd been working hard for five years, growing my business. While I loved the products and services we offered, there was something missing, and I was convinced that Ferriss had put his finger on what it was; I needed to work less and have more adventures!

The 4-Hour Work Week outlines a system for using outsourcing, automation and prioritization to increase your effectiveness and reduce your working hours. For what purpose? So you can spend your time taking extended 3–6 month "mini-retirements" on a regular basis.

I was convinced that this was the answer. I met with my team, and we spent months analyzing, streamlining and automating. By February 2008, I was ready to take my first mini-retirement; a three-month ski-trip to Whistler, Canada – one of the world's premier ski-resorts.

"This is it!" I thought as I booked my tickets. *"Finally, I'm going to have what I've been looking for. I'm going to be fulfilled, peaceful and exhilarated. I'm going to take my skiing to a new level, feel super-successful and have brilliant bragging rights."*

But that's not how it worked out.

After the euphoria of the first week or two on the slopes had passed, I started feeling distracted, uneasy and bored, with a busy mind and sore feet. I was supposed to be on top of the world! Instead, I was in the doldrums. It didn't make sense to me. I'd played the game and won! I should be feeling amazing, but I wasn't. I had the *circumstances* of success, but I wasn't having the *experience* of success.

I flew home six weeks early and went back to the drawing board.

DISTINCTION: Toxic goals vs. Authentic desires

Toxic goals are goals that diminish a person's quality of life from the moment they set them. They reinforce the outside-in misunderstanding and encourage people to exchange a rich experience of the present moment for a superstitious thought; an idealized future concept. Because they promote feelings of dissatisfaction and lack in the present, many people struggle to make progress on **toxic goals**. Those who achieve a **toxic goal** often find that it doesn't deliver the felt experience that they'd hoped for going forward.

Authentic desires are the most natural thing in the world; an expression of your innate clarity, wisdom and well-being. They're part of following your curiosity and fascination. While **toxic goals** are an example of looking outside yourself for something that can only come from inside you, **authentic desires** are things you want for their own sake, for no other reason than wanting them. As a result, there's no sense of angst or lack with **authentic desires**; no sense of striving or *"I'll be happy when..."* When it's an **authentic desire**, you know you'll be fine whether you achieve it or not.

So am I saying you shouldn't have goals?

No, I'm not. Our neurology uses goal-feedback mechanisms to accomplish even the simplest of tasks, such as scratching an itch, brushing your teeth or making a cup of tea. Goals can be really useful tools for focusing your attention, marshalling your resources and measuring progress. But, just like any other tool, improper use can lead to injury.

Toxic goals often take one of the following forms (you'll recognize some of these as having the "hidden hamster wheel" structure):

- I want [*goal*] so I can be [*happy, peaceful, secure, ok*].

- I want [*goal*] or I can't be [*happy, peaceful, secure, ok*].

- I want [*goal*] so I can stop feeling [*unhappy, insecure, not-ok*].

- I want [*goal*] so I will feel [*validated/successful/approved of*].

- I want [*goal*] because I think I *should* want it.

- I want [*goal*] because I don't know what I *really* want.

- I want [*goal*] because I'm *afraid* to go for what I really want.

- I want [*goal*] because I don't want [*consequence*] to happen.

All these goal-structures are based on the misunderstanding that our feelings come from something *other than* thinking in the moment. But it doesn't work that way.

People typically respond to toxic goals in one of two ways. They either:

a) struggle and strive, failing to achieve the toxic goal (sometimes for years), and finally give up with a sense of frustration and hopelessness, or...

b) succeed in achieving the toxic goal, experience an initial rush of euphoria, then feel a sense of emptiness and lack. This is often accompanied by the sentiment *"So that wasn't it either...,"* followed by the setting of yet *another* toxic goal (often "bigger and better" than the last one).

The security blanket

A few years ago, I was working with a client who had set himself a personal goal to raise 2.1 million pounds. I commented that it was a very specific amount, and asked him what he planned to spend it on. He said he didn't want to spend it on *anything*. He went on to explain that he'd calculated 2.1 million pounds as the amount of money he needed to have in his bank account before he could feel a sense of security. Toxic goal alert! It raises an important question:

*"How secure can a person ever feel when they're believing that their security comes from something outside of them; something **other than** THOUGHT in the moment?"*

Many toddlers have a security blanket or teddy bear. This is what psychologists refer to as a "transitional object"; something that "gives" the child a sense of comfort and security in times of change or uncertainty (e.g. bedtime). Of course, we know that the blanket or teddy bear can't actually "give" the child a feeling of security or comfort; that can only come from within the child themselves. It just *seems* to the child as though the feelings come from the transitional object. But it doesn't work that way. It only works one way; inside-out.

I once worked with a multi-millionaire who felt anxious and insecure whenever the stock market dipped. He thought his happiness and security were index-linked! Feelings of security only ever come from your secure thinking, but if a person superstitiously believes that their security comes from money in the bank, they'll see that as a reality.

Money is one of the most misunderstood substances on the planet; so many of us have vast amounts of superstitious thinking about it. But money is just a tool; a means of exchanging value. It can be extremely useful; there are things you can do easily with money that are much more difficult without it. But it's still just a tool, like a hammer or a hairdryer. It has a purpose but, like a hammer or a hairdryer, money can't deliver something beyond the scope of its function. Specifically, it can't give you a feeling of security; that only ever comes from your thinking in the moment.

Reality Check

When I first alert people to the issue of toxic goals, they sometimes object, saying something like *"But if I'm happy, contented, and get my sense of security from within, how am I ever going to be motivated to do anything? If I didn't think my goals would bring me the feelings I want, I won't have any drive."*

One of the great myths of our culture is that if people aren't *unsatisfied*, they won't be motivated to do anything. But it's not true.

Myth: Contentment results in lack of motivation

No it doesn't. In fact, quite the opposite. People who are contented are often highly motivated to create. In Daniel Pink's book *Drive* (a study of motivation), he explodes this myth. He points out that (for instance) money isn't a motivator – that while "not enough" money can demotivate people, big cash incentives actually decrease performance on cognitive and creative tasks. He suggests that in the workplace (for instance), people are most consistently motivated by autonomy, mastery and a sense of purpose. (Of course, you and I know that the only thing that will make someone feel motivated is *motivated thinking*.)

There's nothing wrong with material success – it's perfectly fine. But you're much more likely to enjoy it when you build it on your sense of inner security and peace of mind instead of "mortgaging your well-being" with toxic goals.

Remember: toxic goals are just superstitious thoughts. You weren't born thinking them, and you were motivated to learn to walk and to talk. You were motivated to use your hands, to play and to explore. You were motivated to make and create; to love and connect with other people. And you still are, whether you're already aware of it or not.

A tale of two automobiles

One of my clients, Carl, was thrilled the day he bought his new car. The Mazda MX5 convertible with leather seats and all the trimmings had been a dream of his for ages. But when we met for lunch a couple of weeks later, he was downhearted. He explained that, while he'd been over the moon for the first few days after he bought the car, the initial euphoria had been replaced by a strange emptiness, and a craving for something bigger and better. He told me that he'd thought this car was going to make him happy, but it turned out that he probably needed a Ferrari. As I spoke to Carl about the *"I'll be happy when…"* trap, and explained how THOUGHT creates our experience of reality, something shifted for him. He had an insight, and his experience of the car was trans-formed. The craving disappeared, and was replaced with a lasting appreciation and enjoyment. A few months later, Carl got offered an opportunity in Australia, and delighted in giving the car to his younger brother as a gift. Carl moved to Sydney, where he splits his workdays between consulting in the city and running an online business from his apartment overlooking Bondi Beach.

Allan, a successful business consultant, attended one of my events. During a follow-up conversation, I asked what differences he'd noticed since the workshop. He said *"It's been weird."* When I asked for details, Allan explained that, throughout his career, he'd used various material goals to motivate himself. Even as we spoke, above his desk was a picture of the luxury automobile he'd been planning to treat himself to when he hit his next financial target. *"The strange thing is,"* he said, *"since your workshop, I don't really care about that car anymore. In fact, I think I'd rather get a bicycle and ride to work."* He'd started to see through a misunderstanding, and something shifted for him. Allan was still just as inspired to reach his business goals, but no longer needed the car to motivate him.

Authentic desires

So, if the outside-in misunderstanding sponsors toxic goals, what kind of goals are sponsored by an inside-out understanding of life? How can we relate to goals in a way that is fulfilling, productive and healthy?

Case Study: Authentic desire, vision and direction

Joe Stumpf had spent 20 years building an incredibly successful business, "By Referral Only," providing support to real estate agents and mortgage brokers in the USA. Every month, for the previous two decades, he'd flown to a different town or city to run a three-day "main event"; a boot camp to help agents and brokers start getting their businesses on-track. Not only were these events the first step in Joe's sales and marketing funnel; Joe also saw himself as a torch-bearer, bringing knowledge and hope to people who, when they first met him, were often struggling to make a living. His business specialized in helping them move out of

---

struggle and into stability and success (many of Joe's formerly-struggling clients go on to serve as de facto mentors to others.) Joe asked me to coach him because he was at a point of transition, and was feeling stuck. He was proud of the business he'd created, but he no longer wished to fly from city to city each month. He knew that phase of his business was finished, but didn't know what the next phase was. He wanted a new vision for his business and himself, so I worked with Joe to help him find clarity. He emerged with an inspiring vision for his business, and for his role in it. Joe says *"The insights I gleaned from our session resulted in one of the most important directional shifts of my life."* Joe's business has shifted to not just being a training company, but to also being an information publisher and service provider. It's continued to go from strength to strength, despite the economic downturn. And, just as importantly, Joe's following his heart and living life on his own terms. He recently took on the challenge of being the oldest man ever to survive the civilian version of the Navy SEAL "Hell Week" (at age 54), and he's just written a book called *Willing Warrior*.

One of the great things about authentic desires is that they don't need to be realistic; you want what you want, whether you think it's possible for you or not. When you discover an authentic desire, you may have no idea how you're going to achieve it. That's OK. The Pulitzer-prize-winning author, E.L. Doctorow once said: "Writing is like driving at night in the fog. You can only see as far as your headlights, but you can make the whole trip that way." We can extend the "fog" metaphor by thinking of authentic desire as a beacon in the distance. When you step into the fog of the unknown, and keep moving forward, your wisdom will guide you in discovering the path (the "how").

Reality Check

"What about targets, goals and objectives set by other people; my boss, for instance? He sets me toxic goals all the time, but I don't have the luxury of replacing them with authentic desires."

Another person can set you a goal that you don't *like*, but the only thing that can make it "toxic" is your own superstitious thinking; the idea that your happiness, security or peace of mind is in some way bound up in it. You may say *"But I have to do it or I'll lose my job – it's like having a gun to my head."*

The idea that your happiness, security or well-being are dependent on you keeping your job is a great example of the outside-in misunderstanding. Looking to a job for security is like looking to a toaster for peace of mind; it's not that jobs and toasters aren't useful; they just can't give you what you can only find inside of you. One of the things you'll begin to notice as you continue deepening your understanding of innate thinking is that tasks which used to bother you become less and less of an issue. If you're willing to "make a space" for your authentic desires, and take action, you'll be amazed at where they will lead you.

In 2008, I had a flash of insight; a sudden vision of myself sitting by the ocean with a small group of people, sharing my understanding with them. The vision came with a deep sense of peace, security and clarity. At the time, I had no idea how this vision was going to come about; I wasn't experiencing those qualities for myself, so I wasn't in a position to share them with others. But I trusted this inspiring vision, intuitively feeling its authenticity. I followed my authentic desire, and it led me to the understanding I'm sharing with you now. In 2010, I ran my first *Life Transformation Retreat* in Spain, overlooking the ocean, sharing this understanding with a group of 12 people. The retreats are now a regular event, and will continue to be so for as long as they remain an authentic desire.

Once you realize that you clarity, security and well-being isn't dependent on setting or achieving goals, then you can relax, and allow your wisdom to guide you. Authentic desires will emerge in their own time. As you begin to realize you don't need *anything* to be OK, you also realize there's no urgent need to uncover your authentic desires; they'll come when they come.

In the meantime, stay in the game. 80% of success is showing up, and authentic desires often find you when and where you least expect it.

So, with that in mind, I'd like to take you somewhere very special, to a place that holds the answers to all your questions, and the solutions to all your problems...

---

keep exploring ⠿ connect with others
share your discoveries ⠿ deepen your understanding

Reflection point: As you're reading this now, are there any "toxic goals" that still look like a reality to you? It's ok; they're just an example of habitual thinking. You'll notice that they start to fade as you continue directing your attention away from the products of THOUGHT, and towards what's creating your thoughts. In the meantime, what are some of the authentic desires that you're already starting to become aware of?

Even if you aren't aware of them yet, isn't it nice to know that your authentic desires are already there within you and beginning to emerge? When you find a moment to explore the extra resources for this chapter, you might like to post a list of any toxic goals that are past their sell-by date. And how about starting a list of any authentic desires you're already able to identify? Just use the URL below or scan the QR code to access the resources, post your findings and find out what other people are sharing...

www.ClarityBook.biz/chapter13

14

The Power of Presence

"We convince by our presence."

Walt Whitman, Poet
and journalist

"It's... Uhh... Ahh... Umm..."

The location was St Lucia, and it was the third day of one of my *Life Transformation Retreats*. One of the participants had just had a profound insight (signalled with a loud "OH!" and a look of sudden realization). Everyone in the group turned to him, eager to hear about the pearl of wisdom that had just been revealed to him. He opened his mouth to speak, and said "It's... uhh... ahh... umm..." He stopped, furrowed his brow, then tried again. This time, no sounds came out; his mouth just opened and closed as the expression on his face cycled through a variety of emotions: surprise, confusion, puzzlement, amusement, peace...

His habitual thinking had been massively interrupted; he'd woken up to the present moment.

Being present

Being present is often described as having your attention on what's happening in the present moment. But there's more to it (and less to it) than that. There are many examples where a person is attending to their immediate environment, behaviour or experience, but isn't truly present:

- A business leader may be putting a huge amount of attention on the speech they're making to their team, but not be present.

- A tennis player may be very focused on avoiding mistakes, and on the strengths and weaknesses of the person they're competing against, but not be truly present.

- A person who has a phobic response to a spider may be acutely aware of the sudden change in their thinking and feeling state, but not be at all present.

- A doctor may have their attention highly focused on the patient they're working with, and doing their best to serve them, but not be truly present.

"Present" is whatever is happening moment to moment, *prior to* your habitual thinking.

The grape escape

One morning, before the start of a day's workshop, I was sitting in a reflective state, eating some particularly plump, juicy grapes. As I lifted one of the grapes to my lips, I suddenly "saw" the grape. I mean really saw it!

Time stopped. The world became still and silent. In an instant, I found myself wordlessly fascinated and astonished by the miniature work of "biological engineering" I was holding between my fingers.

It was as though I was seeing a grape for the first time, unencumbered by memories, concepts and other mental clutter. My habitual thinking had paused (temporarily), and I found myself having a more primary experience of life. And what was the natural response to this unmediated perception?

Appreciation, awe, and wonder.

Our experience of life is inherently clear, fulfilling and involving when there's nothing else in the way. What *gets* in the way is our habitual patterns of thinking. For example...

A) A person can be in a situation they might normally describe as "wonderful," but be having an experience that is stressed, anxious or miserable because they've got something on their mind. An all-too-common example of this is when people go on holiday. They can be in the most beautiful environment, with the people they most want to be with, but they find that their work has come on holiday with them, thanks to their habitual patterns of thinking. This is often exacerbated by the proliferation of communications and information technology.

B) By the same token, a person can be in a situation they might normally describe as "boring" or "miserable," but be having an experience that is rich, fulfilling and profound because they've got nothing on their mind. I sometimes enjoy sitting by the ocean, looking out at the waves for 20 or 30 minutes at a time. Ten years ago, I would have had enough of it after two minutes, and felt bored and distracted if I had to stay there. But because I have a lot less on my mind these days, the experience of the waves is rich, absorbing and engaging (except when it's not).

What's the difference between the two situations? Habitual patterns of thought. In situation "A" the person is caught up in their superstitious thinking, while in situation "B" the person has greater clarity; the principle of THOUGHT is creating a rich experience of the moment, relatively unperturbed by superstitious thinking.

Digging, sanding and sweeping

A few years ago, my friends Andy and Cath Duncan invited me to take part in a charity building project they were planning in South Africa. I thought about it. I didn't like being out in very hot sunshine (I prefer the shade), and tended to avoid manual labour unless absolutely necessary. The prospect of spending a week involved in both sounded like a special flavour of hell.

I said I'd do it.

The project was to convert a derelict building into accommodation for staff at a rural hospital. The start of each day's work was the same: my habitual thinking would go into extreme protest, making the experience of whatever I was doing very unpleasant. Then I would start to get more involved in my activity for the day; digging up sprawling inkweed roots, sanding down the walls of the building, sweeping up goat-droppings (each night, the local goat population used the gutted building as a makeshift discotheque).

After between ten and fifteen minutes, I'd notice that my habitual thinking had faded into the background, and that I was having an enjoyable experience; present, peaceful, engaged.

My superstitious thinking calmed down and my mind cleared as I woke up to the present moment.

So, how does our habitual thinking take us *out* of the present moment? By creating THOUGHT-objects that take us into the future or the past. These thoughts can take a variety of forms, for example:

- Toxic goals
- Worrying
- Anxiety
- Daydreaming
- Resentments
- Remembering
- Ruminating
- Judgements
- Imagining
- Planning
- Fear of loss
- Comparing
- Validation-seeking
- Attention-seeking
- etc.

But here's the thing: there is only ever this moment. The present is all there is. The future and the past are THOUGHT-generated illusions; illusions that you only ever *experience* in the present.

Thought Experiment

Try this out: remember an enjoyable experience from the past. 100% of your experience of that memory is taking place in the present moment; none of it is happening in the past. Now imagine something you're going to do in the future. 100% of your experience of that imagined event is taking place in the present moment; none of it is happening in the future. Whether you're remembering the past or imagining the future, it's all taking place in the present. When you find yourself in the "now," it's an indication that you're not caught up in your habitual thinking; you're in the unknown, pointed in the direction of the formless.

Case Study: Grace under pressure

Tim is an entrepreneur with several successful businesses, and was used to experiencing all the stress and pressure that can bring. Then he started exploring *Innate Thinking®*, and found himself becoming increasingly present, patient and resourceful. As he started having insights into where the stress and pressure were *actually* coming from, they began to reduce. He now stays calm in situations that used to aggravate him, and it's paying off; Tim's work involves a lot of high-value negotiations, and his calm new demeanour has been worth many tens of thousands of pounds in deals done and contracts won. And it's equally valuable in situations of growth and crisis. When one of Tim's businesses lost a contract worth 50% of its annual sales, the more traditional reactions of panic and stress were nowhere to be seen. Instead, his calm assessment allowed a rapid and positive response to the challenges posed. Tim was able to reduce the scale of the loss and quickly find replacement orders. Tim says, *"Feeling calm and being able to handle pressure is priceless, but bills don't pay themselves. What's really great is the fact that I can put a financial value on this understanding."*

DISTINCTION: Meditating vs. Meditation

The act of **meditating** is a practice that has one goal; entering a state of **meditation**. **Meditation** is a reflective state that's often accompanied by a sense of clarity and peace of mind, free from superstitious thinking, and resting in the present moment. ("A state of **Meditation"** is another way of describing the reflective states that give rise to the flashes of strategic brilliance mentioned in Chapter 12.)

Contrary to popular opinion, you don't need to be **meditating** in order to enter a state of **meditation**. People find themselves in a state of **meditation** in a variety of situations: going for a walk, listening to classi-cal music, fishing, running, taking a shower, driving, listening to another person, sitting in quiet reflection, reading a book etc.

As you continue exploring innate thinking more deeply, you'll start find-ing your way into a state of **meditation**, free from superstitious think-ing, more and more frequently. So does this mean you'll find yourself cross-legged, chanting "Ommm" in the middle of business-meetings? Fortunately not.

Just as insights are "context-sensitive," so is clarity. The meditative states you find yourself enjoying will be "fit for purpose," bringing you what you need, when you need it.

The athlete's clarity (aka "the zone") when they're performing at their best has a different flavour to the computer programmer's clarity (aka "flow"). While they're both expressions of clarity, they're configured to meet different requirements. They're different again from the tranquil, meditative state that arises when you're getting away from it all, looking out at the waves. But all have three things in common: clarity of mind, access to the resources you need and being present to the moment.

Your deepening understanding of the principles behind innate thinking will bring you more and more fully into the present, with everything you need to respond effectively in the moment.

In Chapter 13, I suggested that the present holds the answers to all your questions, and the solutions to all your problems, and you may be wondering if this bold claim is justified. How is finding your way back to the present going to make a difference to the things that matter in life? Here's how... Do you remember the Bateson quote?

> *"The major problems in the world are the result of the difference between how nature works and the way people think."*

When you're out of our habitual thinking, you're more closely aligned with reality. When you're in the present, you're "before" your habitual thinking, responsive to what's happening, with the clarity that comes from being more deeply connected with life.

A person's *thinking* is what's behind their ability to perceive something as a problem in the first place. When you step into the present, you step out of your habitual ways of seeing a situation. This frees you to tune in to your innate wisdom and see reality more clearly.

Clear mind, more time

One of the things I often hear from my clients when they start exploring *Innate Thinking*® is how much extra time they have.

Whenever a client says this, I make a point of asking what they attribute this extra time to. Their answer usually includes one or more of the points on this list:

- The amount of time they're no longer wasting in insecure, outside-in thinking.

- Having insights that lead to more effective use of their time.

- More intuitive decision making, with less time wasted stressing about choices.

- More elegant, leveraged ways of getting things done and achieving results.

- Better ideas and creative solutions to problems.

- Eliminating tasks that no longer seem important.

- Less time lost to worry and anxiety, more time spent in "flow."

- Getting more from the time they spend; being more productive.

- Better performance, resulting in greater impact, fewer errors and less re-work.

- Less thinking *about* what they're going to do; less procrastination, more action.

- A richer experience of the present moment; getting more "juice" from their day.

> *The outside-in misunderstanding is the biggest time-thief there is. If it wasn't for our superstitious thinking, we'd discover that every day brings a 1:1 match of time and enterprise. When we're present, with a clear mind, we have what we need for the task at hand. We intuitively know when to pause and when to press on; when to rest and when to proceed...*

This *doesn't* necessarily mean that on a daily basis you're going to work out at the gym, answer all your email, and clear your to-do list. Your habitual thoughts about what you *think* you should be doing is not necessarily part of this 1:1 match of time and enterprise. But as you continue to explore *Innate Thinking®*, you'll discover the implicit connection between presence, performance and perfect timing.

When you return to the present, you step out of the outside-in misunderstanding about how life works. The idea that your well-being is being held hostage by a given problem or issue often drops away, and clarity emerges. Strange as it may seem, you discover that all is well in this moment.

Reality Check

You may be saying *"What about problems that need solving urgently? If I lose my job, clarity isn't going to help me pay the bills!"* Life has its ups and downs. While some hardships are inevitable for each of us, there are two things that mean we can deal with any situation we encounter:

1. *We each have within us a source of security, well-being and resilience.*

2. *We each have within us a source of clarity, wisdom and guidance.*

In fact, these things aren't just within you; they *are* you. Clarity, wisdom and resilience are your nature. The knowledge that clarity comes from within, combined with your innate guidance system gives you everything you need to deal with the ups and downs of life.

All over the world, on a daily basis, people lose jobs, get divorced, lose loved-ones and get injured. We all get our share of hurts, hardships and disappointments. People's responses to these misfortunes range from denial, trauma and shutdown to reflection, acceptance and bounce-back. When you have clarity, you realize you have what you need to respond appropriately and deal with what comes your way.

A lot of the things that people experience as "problems" are grounded in superstitious thinking; an outside-in misunderstanding of reality. The stress and anxiety inherent in this misunderstanding has people creating problems where there are none, and responding unresourcefully to the things that *do* need dealing with.

But there's something utterly reliable that everyone's got, but that very few people *realize* they have. Something that means you don't have to worry; that you've got what it takes to handle what comes your way...

---

keep exploring ❖ connect with others
share your discoveries ❖ deepen your understanding

Reflection point: *"If it wasn't for our superstitious thinking, we'd discover that every day brings a 1:1 match of time and enterprise." Consider this curious statement. Then reflect on the fact that, if it wasn't for your superstitious thinking, you'd find every activity you undertake to be engaging, absorbing and fulfilling. Even accounts, filing and doing the dishes! And when you'd finished for the day, you'd be relaxed and clear-headed. And while I don't know anyone who experiences this 100% of the time, isn't it nice to know that's on offer at the level of principle?*

This one's really worth sitting with. It can be very liberating to realize that, in the big scheme of things, you have exactly enough time to do what you need to do, without stress, worry or pressure. Whenever you're ready, scan the QR code with your smartphone or type the URL into your browser to enjoy more resources to help you deepen your understanding. Please post your comments, share with your friends and connect with the new people you'll meet here as you keep exploring...

www.ClarityBook.biz/chapter14

15

Resilience

*"Our greatest glory is not in never falling,
but in rising every time we fall."*

Confucius, Philosopher

"There's no place like home... there's no place like home..."

In *The Wizard of Oz*, the heroine (Dorothy, played by Judy Garland) gets caught in a tornado, and wakes up in the strange land of Oz. She's desperate to find her way home to Kansas, and goes on a quest to meet the wizard who she believes holds the key to her return.

At the end of the story, Dorothy discovers that she has the power she needs *within* her. She taps her ruby slippers together, repeats the phrase *"There's no place like home"* and wakes up in her bed, surrounded by her family. Dorothy doesn't believe them when they first tell her the adventure in Oz was a nightmare. She protests that it was a real place, but they reassure her that she never left her home; that it was just a dream...

We've all had the experience of waking up from a dream so realistic that we thought it had actually happened; felt the sense of gratitude and relief as the racing pulse of nightmare gives way to the reality of the here and now. The dream-reality seems so real that we mistake it for a *material* reality. But all along, the dreamer is tucked up in bed, sleeping soundly, perfectly safe.

Touching the void

The nerve-shredding documentary, *Touching the Void*, tells the story of Joe Simpson and Simon Yates, two climbers who made the first ever ascent of the west face of Siula Grande in the Peruvian Andes. On their way back down, Simpson fell and broke his leg. It was a death sentence. Simpson told Yates to go on without him, but Yates refused, instead choosing to lower him down the steep, snow-covered slope at the end of a long rope. After hours of painstaking descent, Yates suddenly felt the rope go taught; Simpson had fallen and was hanging off the edge of a cliff!

Yates was stuck in a nightmarish dilemma. Simpson's weight was slowly pulling Yates free from his belay point in the snow. If Yates kept holding on, he'd be pulled off the mountain, but the only alternative was to cut the rope.

Finally Yates made a decision; he cut the rope and Simpson plummeted into a crevasse where he lay shivering and alone, without food and seriously injured.

When Yates climbed down and saw the crevasse, he assumed that Simpson was dead, and continued down the mountain. But Simpson was alive. Over the next three days, in a feat of resilience that can only be described as heroic, Simpson hopped, crawled and dragged himself over treacherous terrain, arriving at the base camp only hours before Yates was planning to leave.

In Simpson's description of the incident, he explained that it wasn't "him" that brought him down the mountain; it was as if someone else was doing it. That "someone else" was his innate resilience, a power we all have within us.

Sleepwalking

A huge number of people today "sleepwalk" their way through life, innocently hypnotized by the outside-in misunderstanding. Occasionally they wake up to a deeper, more profound experience in the moment, but usually attribute it to some aspect of their circumstances before going back to business as usual. In fact, we all "sleepwalk" some of the time, no matter how "awake" we may be. We all fall into the outside-in trance on a regular basis – that's part of what it is to be human.

We walk around with our heads in the clouds, lost in a world of our habitual thinking. But, all the time, the ground we are walking on is a world of clarity and depth of experience; a more profound sense of peace and understanding. No matter how real and compelling our personal realities sometimes seem, a world of deeper experience is just below the surface, in every moment.

Sometimes, the outside-in hypnosis is so powerful that it seems unbelievable that our clarity and peace of mind could be so close by. We mistakenly believe that our ability to reconnect with them can be influenced by material-world factors; factors such as the length of time we've been thinking and feeling in a certain way, the intensity of our feelings or the difficulty we've had solving a problem until now.

We assume our thought-forms have the same qualities as the material world, but they don't. They're made of THOUGHT, the reality principle; fleeting and ephemeral, the same thing *dreams* are made of. Your clarity and well-being is always there, always within reach, no matter how distant it may have seemed until now.

A tale of two burglaries

Back in 2006, I caught a young man trying to rob my offices. He managed to slip out of the fire escape, and I gave chase, but he outran me. Despite the fact that he hadn't managed to steal anything, I was upset and, as the day went on, I got more and more angry. Finally, I called my mentor, Terry, and asked for his help. I said I couldn't understand why I was getting so angry, but I wanted it to stop. What he said will stay with me forever.

He said, *"You've got a business model, and that young man has a business model. Your business model has certain advantages and disadvantages, and so does his. For a start, his model probably involves him running away from angry people more often than yours does."*

In the blink of an eye, I saw the whole situation differently. My spirits rose and I started feeling peaceful. I was no longer angry at the young man.

Our clarity and peace of mind have a natural buoyancy. Like a football being held underwater, as soon as you let go, it rises to the surface. It doesn't matter how long you've been holding it there, or how much effort you've put into it; the moment you let go, its natural buoyancy begins to lift it. And, just as a football's natural buoyancy is an implication of the principle of gravity, your clarity and resilience are implications of the principles of innate thinking.

Two years later, I arrived at my home to find the front door hanging open; my laptop and mobile phone had been stolen. To my amazement, I was calm, philosophical and practical. I did what I needed to do, without fear, anger or agitation. The insight I'd had two years previously was still serving me.

When we're lost in superstitious thinking, we sometimes experience feelings of worry, agitation, urgency etc. Due to a trick of the mind, we tend to "blame" those low feelings on something *other* than our thinking. The moment we do that, we also give our power away, and feel we urgently need to solve our problems, achieve our goals, and make changes in our lives.

The worse we feel, the more urgent and compelling those external changes can seem.

But, as clarity emerges, we wake up into a deeper, more connected experience of life. Suddenly the things we'd been perceiving as problems look different; they disappear, we see obvious solutions, or just feel confident that we'll find a way forward. Our creativity comes to the surface, and our natural resourcefulness and resilience come into play. We intuitively know that we'll be OK no matter what, and that we can trust our wisdom to guide us.

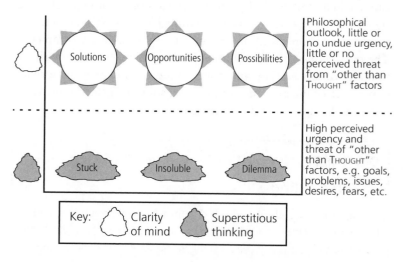

Figure 15.1 The Clarity of Mind Index

Reality Check

Am I suggesting that you stick your head in the sand and ignore your problems? No! But I *am* suggesting that your ability to *perceive* something as a problem in the first place is an expression of your habitual thinking and level of understanding. As you see the situation more clearly, everything looks different, including what you'd been perceiving as a problem.

We've all experienced this. We struggle with a problem for hours, days or even longer, then one morning we wake up and either a) We no longer see it as a problem or b) We see a solution that seems so obvious, we can't believe we didn't see it before. You are innately resilient; clarity and peace of mind are always there, just a thought away.

And what may seem counterintuitive in our modern world of multi-tasking, instant messaging, and 24-hour opening is this: you can live in and from clarity, insight and a more profound felt experience of life. Everyone gets hoodwinked by superstitious thinking from time to time, and no one gets to avoid its lows completely. The outside-in misunderstanding is compelling, and our clarity of mind inevitably goes up and down. But greater clarity and a richer experience of life are our natural state, so we can start to gravitate towards that as our default setting.

DISTINCTION: Clarity of mind vs. Clarity of understanding

We all experience **clarity of mind** from time to time; present and in the moment, with our heads free from superstitious thinking. While the flow states regularly enjoyed by athletes, musicians and dancers (among others) are a familiar example of **clarity of mind**, we *all* experience this in different ways and at various times in our own lives. **Clarity of mind** is, by its nature, fleeting; no one has it all the time.

Clarity of understanding is the degree to which you insightfully understand the inside-out nature of reality; the realization that 100% of your felt experience of life is coming from THOUGHT in the moment. The fact that you're reading this book means that you're in the process of becoming one of those exceptional people who has **clarity of understanding** about the inside-out nature of life. **Clarity of understanding** is permanent. Once you experience an increase in your level of understanding, you never lose it. You'll lose *sight* of it from time to time (if you're anything like me, it'll be on a daily basis), but your insights into the inside-out nature of life are still there within you; it's only a matter of time before your wisdom reminds you and guides you back to clarity.

Of course, we all have an *innate* understanding of the inside-out nature of life at the core of our consciousness; it's what we're "made of" at the most essential level. So, as you keep looking in this direction, and allowing insight to dissolve the outside-in misunderstanding, it's inevitable that your increasing **clarity of understanding** will continue rising. And the higher it rises, the more **clarity of mind** you'll find yourself experiencing.

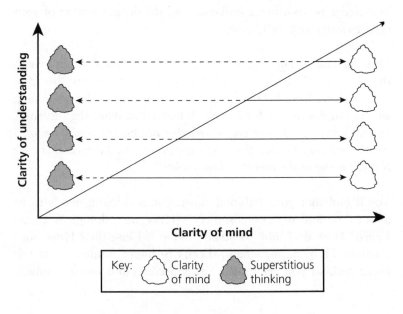

Figure 15.2 Clarity of Mind vs. Clarity of Understanding

Life is not a problem to be solved

The philosopher Kierkegaard wisely said that life is not a problem to be solved; that it's a mystery to be experienced. When we lose our clarity of mind, we innocently look at life as a series of problems to be solved and goals to be achieved. But the agitation and urgency are actually our wisdom signalling us...

- reminding us that we're feeling our thinking...

- pointing us in the direction of clarity, possibility and peace of mind...

- guiding us to look away from the *content* of our experience, and towards the "unknown" of that which is *creating* our experience of life; the principles of innate thinking.

As you start to see how the principles of innate thinking are playing out in your life (and always have been), you can start living more and more in clarity, insight and a deeper felt experience of life. You'll still have your ups and downs but, behind them, is the knowledge of your inner resilience and the default-setting of your innate clarity and well-being.

Near the end of *The Wizard of Oz*, Glinda the good witch reveals that Dorothy has always had the power to get home, but that she wouldn't have believed it if she'd been told at the beginning; she had to discover it for herself. When asked what she's learned, Dorothy says *"If I ever go looking for my heart's desire again, I won't look any further than my own backyard. Because if it isn't there, I never really lost it to begin with!"*

You'll find that your habitual superstitious thinking tends to be about "me and my circumstances" (How am I doing? What do I need? How do I look to others? What if I lose this? How can I get that? I'll be happy when.../I can't be happy because... etc.). It looks real, so you get fooled into searching and seeking outside yourself for something that's already there within you. When you get caught up in your habitual thinking, you innocently mistake it for a material reality. But it's not a reality – it's just a dream.

The dream-reality seems so real that you mistake it for a material reality. But, all along, the dreamer is tucked up in bed, sleeping soundly, perfectly safe.

Everyone has dreams of isolation and insecurity from time to time but, in any moment, you can wake up to the reality of who you really are...

- you are the dreamer...

- you are the thinker...

- you are not the dream; you are what's *creating* the dream...

- you are not your thoughts; you are what's *creating* the thoughts...

> *You are not your experience;*
> *you are what's creating your experience;*
> MIND, *the power principle,*
> *the "intelligent energy" behind life...*

> *In any moment, you can wake up to the truth of who you are,*
> *and live life more fully from clarity, insight and peace of mind...*

So, if the dream of isolation is an illusion, what's the deeper reality behind life? If you are the dreamer, perfectly safe, what's the truth of the domain you're resting in? And what awaits you as you continue waking up?

keep exploring ⁖ connect with others
share your discoveries ⁖ deepen your understanding

Reflection point: *"Your clarity and peace of mind have a natural buoyancy. Like a football being held underwater; as soon as you let go, it rises to the surface."* This emotional buoyancy is an implication of the principles of innate thinking. Isn't it a relief to realize that clarity, security and peace of mind are always on-hand? Ready to rise to the surface, no matter what, as soon as you insightfully realize that you're feeling your thinking in the moment?

Resilience is innate; it's there in everyone, but most people don't understand this. As you start to see this as a fact for yourself, the whole game changes. Don't just take my word for it; have a look at what other people are saying about this: scan the QR code with your smartphone or type the URL into your browser. You'll find additional resources to help deepen your understanding, as well as opportunities to share what you're uncovering…

www.ClarityBook.biz/chapter15

16

Connection and Relationships

"Social media has transformed our world into one great big small town, dominated, as all vibrant towns used to be, by the strength of relationships, the currency of caring, and the power of word of mouth."

Gary Vaynerchuk, Entrepreneur and social media specialist

"Make me one with everything..."

The punchline to the old joke about the Buddhist and the hotdog vendor casts a light on one of life's most persistent illusions. It certainly *looks* like we're separate from each other, and from the natural world. But, strange as it may seem, there's a way in which separation is an illusion. In reality, the fact that everything is made of energy means, in a very empirical sense, that we are all connected; with one another and with the rest of the universe.

We don't need anyone or anything to "make us" one with everything. We already *are* one with everything; we always have been and we always will be. However...

Superstitious thinking gives us the experience of separation.

As we get caught up in habitual thinking we experience the illusion of separation from other people, and from life. The more superstitious thinking we're in, the more separate we feel.

And what does this have to do with connection and relationships?

*The true source of loneliness, isolation and most conflict
is the belief that we're feeling something other than our thinking;*

*that we're at the mercy of a world "out there"
with power over how we feel.*

*Connection, intimacy and love are what's already there
for us when there's nothing else in the way...*

And what gets in the way? Habitual patterns of superstitious thinking.

DISTINCTION: Separation vs. Connection

An example of the **separation**-illusion taken to an extreme is the person suffering from clinical paranoia, seeing enemies "out to get them" wherever they look. A sense of loneliness, isolation or hostility are characteristics of many mental illnesses, but we all feel that way to some degree when we're lost in the illusion of our habitual, superstitious thinking.

A common example of the experience of **connection** is when two people are deeply in love. Much of their superstitious thinking drops away (albeit temporarily), and they experience a sense of unity and **connection**, with the other person and often with life in general (*"It seems like all the colours are brighter, and the world is a wonderful place!"*).

Then, they go outside-in again, blaming their loving feelings on the object of their affection (*"You complete me"*); but the feelings of love, clarity and **connection** are our natural state when superstitious thinking isn't getting in the way. The flip side of this is what happens when people fall *out* of love with each other; they blame their partner for their *unpleasant* feelings, their heads fill up, and they feel separate and isolated.

Of course, you don't have to be in love with someone to feel a **connection** with them. **Connection** is natural between people when our habitual thinking isn't getting in the way.

And **connection** is worth something. In addition to the fact that it's natural and feels good, **connection** opens up a conduit for effective communication. When another person feels connected to you, they're much more likely to see where you're coming from, hear what you have to say and be impacted by what you're sharing with them.

Listening to be impacted

I was recently at a meeting where one of the participants asked for help with an issue he'd been struggling with. He gave a brief outline of the problem (he'd been having trouble finding the right direction for his business) then the other participants started jumping in with solutions. I just listened. When the first round of solution-giving was over, I asked if it would be OK to do some exploring. He and the other participants agreed, so I asked him questions, then listened as deeply as I could to his answers. A feeling of connection started to develop, and he became reflective. All of a sudden, his face lit up. *"I need to have more passion and adventure in what I'm doing,"* he said. Over the weeks and months that followed, he started making the necessary changes to move in this new direction. When you listen deeply, and allow a connection to emerge, the resulting conversations can be profound, creative and extremely useful.

The London Olympics

During the London Olympics, a curious phenomenon took place; all over the country, people's moods lifted. I was interviewed by Sky Radio News to give my perspective. At one point, the interviewer asked why communities were coming together around the Olympics, and why people felt more connected to one another. I said that feelings of connection and belonging are natural for people when they're not lost in isolated, stressful thinking; that when people feel more connected, they have a greater sense of well-being. I explained that there's nothing inherent in the nature of communities (or events such as the Olympics) that has us feeling connected or disconnected; it's always down to our thinking.

It looked like the Olympics was making people feel more optimistic and connected, but the optimism and connection they were feeling is natural for people when they're paying less attention to superstitious thinking.

As your understanding of innate thinking increases,
superstitious thinking falls away
and you start experiencing greater connection...

Case Study: Rapid development

Ian works as a programme manager for a disruptive online business. The company employs 400 people and has an aggressive development schedule, releasing new versions of its online services several times per month. Ian runs two teams of extremely bright, talented individuals (many of them honours graduates from Oxford and Cambridge), and is responsible for new software releases. It's a fast-moving enterprise, using agile, "just in time" development processes.

Before Ian started learning about *Innate Thinking*®, the high-pressure, high-speed environment was stressful and hyper-busy, making life difficult for him and his team members. There were entrenched viewpoints and antagonistic differences of opinion. Communications broke down easily; project timescales were affected and the results were less than ideal. Ian tried to use various techniques to get people aligned, but nothing seemed to be working.

Then Ian joined one of my programmes and started learning the principles of innate thinking. Over the past 12 months, a trust has developed between the individual team-members, and with the business stakeholders. He reports that *"an understanding of innate thinking brings a psychologically healthy and emotionally mature approach to working in teams."* There's more engagement, honesty and open communications. Ian went on to explain that, while his team still apply analytical thinking and solid business experience, innate thinking provides a stable foundation for those efforts. Ian says *"It's still hard work, and issues come up, but they get sorted out quickly now."*

A clear example is product managers, under a lot of pressure to deliver projects to a deadline. When product managers get stressed, the whole team suffers; before long, developers start turning up late for work, taking long lunches and getting into "bitch sessions." Morale and productivity fall, and communication starts breaking down, making the deadline an impossible target. Ian says, *"Before I understood innate thinking, I would try using a variety of persuasion techniques to reason with the product managers but, if anything, it made them more stressed."*

That's all changed since Ian got an understanding of *innate thinking*. Recently, a product manager came to him, visibly stressed about a deadline. Ian explains, *"I felt a sense of inner calm and outer urgency, and that showed up in my communication. We quickly moved beyond the perceived stress of the situation to brainstorming how to resolve things in the best way possible. We came up with some new ideas from that place of calm urgency and proceeded straight away to engaging other people we would need to unblock our delivery problem."*

The delivery team were protected from the emotional stress of the product manager, and they got the problem unblocked within a day. This, along with other quick and calm responses, contributed to getting the whole project completed ahead of schedule and under budget.

In the past, a dispute between a team member and a business stakeholder raged on for a year, and was only resolved when the team member was physically moved out of the team. In contrast, a recent dispute that had the potential to go the same way was solved by Ian over a few conversations in less than 48 hours; now the two people work well together. Ian explains, *'There's a better feeling in the team, with more learning during our weekly review sessions. People really listen to each other these days."* The team members are more playful, yet both teams have hit all their deadlines, with high-quality results. Ian conservatively estimates the bottom-line impact of what he's been learning at over £300,000 in improved delivery times alone.

The impact of learning *Innate Thinking®* has also been significant for Ian personally. He says, *"I used to bring my work home with me, and there was a lot of pressure and stress. I'd have sleepless nights, and my wife would get annoyed because I was thinking about work when we were together."* While Ian still gets caught up in his thinking from time to time, it's much less frequent, and never lasts as long. His sleep is better, and he rarely thinks about work outside of working hours these days. He's more reflective, and has become a reliable source of creative solutions and fresh perspectives. He describes himself as *"in the zone"* for much of his working day, and his reputation is spreading; other employees have started actively seeking him out for help with conflicts, problems and issues.

Two worlds in one

Imagine you're watching a film at the cinema. As you look at the characters on the screen, you experience them as separate people – figures moving against a background. Our ability to experience them as distinct from each other (and from the setting) is what allows us to transform the patterns of light on the screen into individual characters. This in turn allows us to experience the drama of the film as it unfolds.

But the seemingly separate figures on the screen are actually part of an unbroken continuum of light and shadow. The distinctions between the characters, and between figure and ground, are mind-made illusions, generated from within us. The same goes for all the feelings we experience as we watch the movie.

*The film is neutral; 100% of our experience of
(and response to) the film arises from within us.*

Now, let's go one step further. The flow of images on the screen is only there because light is shining from a projector at the back of the cinema. The patterns of light on the screen have no existence independent of the projector and the reel of film it's playing. Form and formless are one, a unified whole. Switch off the light and the movie disappears from the screen.

The tangible illusion of the film on the screen has no existence separate from the (relatively) intangible reality of the light shining from the projector.

It's the same with us. Our experience of the world of form (including each other) is a tangible illusion; tangible, but not real. The principles of innate thinking represent a deeper reality; intangible, but real, giving rise to the tangible illusion of the material world. And, just as the images on the screen have no existence independent of the light from the projector, the world of form has no existence independent of the formless energy behind life. Form and formless are one, a unified whole.

Just as a wave has no existence separate from the ocean, the material world of form in all its glory has no existence separate from the formless energy behind life. Leading physicists such as David Bohm (one of the pioneers of quantum mechanics) acknowledge that an understanding of the oneness of life is essential for science and humanity to continue evolving.

In a dream, your mind creates and perceives a world...

When you're asleep and dreaming, everything in the dream arises from inside you. All the characters, environments and situations are created using innate thinking, arising from within your consciousness.

It's the same when you're awake. Remember: 100% of your experience of the world "outside" of you is actually taking place *inside* of you, generated from deep within your awareness. The principles of innate thinking give rise to our experience of reality. Our personal thoughts, perceptions and self-images are like waves; we can notice them, obsess about them, even take ownership of them. But they have no existence separate from the whole. They don't "belong" to us any more than a droplet of water "belongs" to a given whirlpool or wave.

As our clarity of understanding increases, something amazing begins to happen. Life starts looking less complex, and we begin to see a simplicity behind many of the challenges people face. In fact, in a world that appears beset by a dizzying array of complex issues and seemingly impossible problems, there's a realization that can offer genuine hope and practical solutions...

keep exploring ⟡ connect with others
share your discoveries ⟡ deepen your understanding

Reflection point: "Connection, intimacy and love are what's already there for us when there's nothing else in the way." What would it mean for you and your various relationships if this were true? Connection is like WD-40 for relationships; it lubricates and unsticks them, making them rich and fluid. What are some of the relationships you can already imagine enjoying more fully now that you're starting to see this more clearly?

A great way to play with this is to start connecting with people, and you can do it right away. Just scan the QR code with your smartphone, or enter the URL into your browser to access the additional resources for this chapter and get connected. "Read for an insight" as you have a look at what others are posting, and start sharing your own insights, discoveries and a-has…

www.ClarityBook.biz/chapter16

PART THREE

The Way Forward

17

There's Only One Problem

*"When I am working on a problem,
I never think about beauty
but when I have finished,
if the solution is not beautiful,
I know it is wrong."*

R. Buckminster Fuller,
Designer and inventor

"Behind the London riots a multitude of causes..."

The Euronews headline from August 9, 2011 attempted to make sense of the riots that had started that week in London, then spread to other cities in the UK. The TV and newspapers were awash with people (ranging from local teenagers to police and government ministers) giving their opinions on what had caused the riots. The "causes" they identified included:

- the tragic shooting of Mark Duggan by police marksmen
- budget cuts and the removal of social programs
- economic and social inequality
- gangs and gang culture
- poor parenting
- social media and mobile phone technology
- moral breakdown
- poor police response
- consumerism
- a criminal underclass
- unemployment
- etc.

In response to this litany of causes came a variety of proposed solutions. The British Prime Minister, David Cameron, promised an "all-out war on gangs and gang culture." Police responded by arresting 200 gang leaders; but the strategy backfired, creating a dangerous power vacuum. Younger, more volatile gang-members stepped in to fill their shoes, leading to an increase in violence, mayhem and chaos.

But what if this dizzying array of societal, family and individual "causes" were actually not *causes, but effects; the emergent properties of a single, underlying cause?*

The lime solution

During the early 1800s, countless women were dying of puerperal fever, a bacterial infection contracted during childbirth. At the time, the illness was attributed to a mind-boggling variety of causes (ranging from bad smells and "atmospheres" to overcrowding, posture during labour and psychological factors), with an equally wide variety of measures taken to try and prevent its spread.

In the 1840s, a Hungarian doctor, Ignaz Semmelweis, noticed that women who gave birth at home, in the midwives' ward or even in the *street* had a much lower incidence of puerperal fever than those who gave birth in the doctors' ward of his hospital. He had a sudden insight: the illness was being spread by something that couldn't be seen; something on the hands and instruments of the doctors.

In May of 1847, Semmelweis ordered that all doctors in his hospital wash their hands in a chlorinated lime solution before contact with the patients. The rate of puerperal fever fell from 18% to less than 3%.

The theories of the day had identified dozens of "causes," but there was in fact just one cause: germs and bacteria on the unwashed hands and instruments of the doctors.

Today, every doctor knows the importance of "scrubbing up," wearing correct surgical attire and sterilizing their instruments. One of the legacies of Semmelweis' discovery is that most people today survive routine surgery most of the time.

Semmelweis was less fortunate; despite the massive success of the procedures he instituted, his discoveries disagreed with the medical theories of the day. The medical orthodoxy thought Semmelweis' discovery was too simplistic, lacking in credibility and offending their sensibilities (the doctors didn't like the implication that their hands were dirty). He was at first ridiculed, then violently opposed, losing his job and being committed to a mental asylum where he died in 1865 of septicaemia. Semmelweis' practice of hand-washing didn't become widespread until after his death.

Today, "the Semmelweis reflex" is the name given to the knee-jerk rejection of new information because it disagrees with an existing orthodoxy, belief-set or paradigm.

First ridicule... then violent opposition... followed by widespread acceptance.

But is it truly credible that a single cause is responsible for the London riots, just as a single cause was responsible for puerperal fever? If so, what could possibly explain such a diverse and complex array of effects?

A superstition. A misunderstanding. The misguided belief that we're feeling something other than THOUGHT. Think about it: when a person believes they live in an outside-in world, they're confused about where their feelings come from.

- If a person thinks their security, happiness and well-being comes from amassing money and wealth, then they're likely to become *greedy*.

- If a person thinks their agitated feelings are caused by other people, then they're likely to experience *resentment, hostility* and other *relationship problems*.

- If a person's habitual thinking is standing between them and their deeper feelings of peace and well-being, then they're likely to be *unhappy*.

- If a person doesn't understand that 100% of their feelings are coming from their thinking in the moment, then *stress* is a strong possibility.

- If a person thinks their security comes from money, and their money supply starts looking unstable, then *anxiety* and *neediness* are understandable responses.

- If a person doesn't realize that they have a source of wisdom within them, and makes important decisions when they're clouded with superstitious thinking, they're going to make some *bad decisions.*

- If a person doesn't realize that they are profoundly resilient, and they see trouble on the horizon, then they're likely to *worry.*

It doesn't take a huge leap of creativity to trace most of the day's news topics to a small number of culprits: neediness, greed, anxiety, stress, anger, resentment and lack of wisdom. And all these culprits are symptoms of a single problem: superstitious thinking springing from the outside-in misunderstanding.

The theories of the day had identified dozens of "causes," but there was in fact just one cause…

Everyone wants to have a more connected, vibrant and fulfilling experience of life, whether they realize it or not. When we think that our felt experience is *caused* by external circumstances, we'll do almost *anything* to bring those external circumstances into being (e.g. the family man who torpedoes his career, wrecks his marriage and drains his bank account to run off with his secretary, because he believes that she's the source of his happiness and well-being). When we think that our felt experience is *threatened* by external circumstances, we'll do almost anything to avoid them (**e.g. the number of people who would rather die than stand up in front of a group and speak in public**).

As people begin realigning with the inside-out nature of life, they naturally start living from a more alive, more profound felt experience. It becomes your "home base;" when habitual thinking takes you away from that deeper experience of life, it's rarely long before wisdom wakes you up to the fact that you're feeling your thinking, and the system continues self-correcting.

When clarity of mind is grounded in clarity of understanding, it's the natural source of the behaviours traditionally associated with "high character." As you start to insightfully see the inside-out nature of reality, and reconnect with that more profound, more alive felt experience of life, you naturally start responding to situations with clarity, wisdom and integrity.

Reality Check

You may be saying *"What about things like natural disasters, unavoidable accidents, diseases and dementia? There are lots of problems that aren't down to superstitious thinking!"*

True. Life has its ups and downs, and no one gets through it without their share of challenges. Seeing the inside-out nature of reality and living from a clearer, more profound felt experience of life won't stop that. But it gives us a) the resilience to know we can deal with whatever comes our way, and b) the wisdom, clarity and creativity to make a difference in our own lives and in the lives of others going forward.

*It turns out that life is less about what happens to you,
and more about how you relate to it...*

In the past 100 years alone, insight and creativity has resulted in discoveries which have made a massive difference in the lives of millions. Alexander Fleming's discovery of penicillin in 1928 has resulted in the lives of countless people being saved.

But what if there were a kind of "penicillin for the mind" that could have as dramatic an effect on your clarity, your character and your behaviour as antibiotics have had on bacterial infection?

**keep exploring ⁙ connect with others
share your discoveries ⁙ deepen your understanding**

Reflection point: What happens when you consider the possibility that the vast majority of the problems faced by society, businesses and individuals are the result of a single cause? A misunderstanding of the nature of THOUGHT?

It's a big idea, isn't it? Could it really be that simple? Yes. Take a few moments to consider the implications of this. Then go one step further, and consider what the world will look like when we start seeing through the misunderstanding en masse. When you're ready, take a moment to share your ideas and explore the extra resources by scanning the QR code below, or entering the URL into a browser. Try not to become *too* optimistic as you speculate on just how amazing the world will be once we're no longer hamstrung by superstitious thinking...

www.ClarityBook.biz/chapter17

18

Penicillin for the Mind

....

"No problem can be solved from the same level of consciousness that created it."

Albert Einstein, Physicist,
winner of the Nobel Prize
in Physics, 1921

"There's nothing in this world that you can't turn into heroin..."

During an unexpectedly moving scene in the comedy *Get Him to the Greek* (2010, Universal Pictures), drug-addicted rock star Aldous Snow (played by Russell Brand) tries to convince his ex-girlfriend to get back together with him. She explains that she's drug-free, and that the past few months have been the happiest of her life. He protests that he was clean for seven years when they were together. She replies "And you did yoga for five hours a day. That's mental! There's nothing in this world that you can't turn into heroin."

"Symptom substitution" is widely accepted in the world of traditional addiction treatment. The smoker gives up cigarettes but starts eating chocolate. The reformed cocaine addict becomes a workaholic. The alcoholic stops drinking and starts compulsively attending meetings. The surface behaviour has changed, often to something less damaging, but the habitual thought patterns (and the consciousness behind them) remain the same. By the same token, we can all think of examples of people who have had a sudden insight; a change of heart that dramatically impacts their life...

- The alcoholic who experiences a "moment of clarity," stops drinking for good, and becomes a valuable member of their community.

- The smoker who suddenly decides that "enough is enough," and easily gives up a habit that they were previously enslaved by.

- The workaholic businessman who has a heart attack, massively re-evaluates his priorities, downsizes and starts working a four-hour day so he can spend more time with his family.

History also shows us examples of these "moments of truth," from AA founder Bill Wilson's spiritual awakening, to the enlightenment experiences that led martial artist Morihei Ueshiba to create *aikido*.

These changes of heart are often regarded as psychological anomalies, sometimes labelled as "spontaneous remission" and given no further attention. Yet they are examples of a natural quality that we all have:

The capacity for an increase in our clarity of understanding; a rise in our level of consciousness.

While the examples above are dramatic upheavals, we all experience increases in consciousness from time to time. Sometimes it happens "out of the blue," while at other times it's from within a more structured context (the stated purpose of AA's famous 12 steps, for example, is for the alcoholic to have a "spiritual awakening" – an increase in consciousness that transforms their experience of life, including their behaviour).

The infinite elevator

Imagine a sturdy, see-through elevator running up the side of an infinitely tall skyscraper at the centre of a crowded metropolis. When you first step into the elevator, all you can see is the cars at street level and the buildings that surround you.

As the elevator begins to move, you start rising above the smaller buildings, and your sight line becomes less cluttered. The cars appear to grow smaller and smaller, and you can see the rooftops of the neighbouring office blocks. Soon, all but the tallest buildings are disappearing beneath you, and you can see far into the distance.

You admire the gentle transition as the population becomes less dense; from high-rises, to low-rises, to suburbs to countryside. As you continue your upward journey, the details of the city streets shrink into invisibility, and your eye is drawn to the sweep of the horizon. Eventually you start to become aware of the curvature of the Earth.

Your consciousness is like this infinite elevator. A rise in consciousness means an increase in clarity of understanding that brings you peace, perspective and greater clarity of mind.

The principle of CONSCIOUSNESS brings your thinking to life. When you experience a rise in your consciousness, the habits of thinking you previously experienced as a reality suddenly start losing their power. As your consciousness continues rising, you become more and more able to see your THOUGHT-generated experiential realities for the illusions that they are.

A rise in consciousness means a permanent increase in your clarity of understanding...

Penicillin for the mind

A rise in consciousness is like a kind of "penicillin for the mind." Penicillin can help our bodies to heal infection by inhibiting the growth and spread of illness-causing bacteria. Similarly, a rise in consciousness can transform how we relate to (and can even eliminate) huge amounts of habitual thinking. Just as penicillin acts wherever in the body it's needed, a rise in consciousness goes to wherever it's needed in a person's psyche. A person whose consciousness rises often experiences an "across the board" increase in well-being, with issues they'd been perceiving as problems suddenly reducing in intensity, or even disappearing...

Case Study: Fear of conflict and public speaking

Tiffany was afraid to express her point of view during meetings at work, particularly if there was negativity, or if she disagreed with the points others were making. She came to one of my programmes, and we chatted about *Innate Thinking*® over lunch. The following week she found herself able to speak freely during her team meeting, even though she knew other people disagreed with her. She even gave a presentation to the group (something she'd been avoiding doing for months due to a fear of public speaking). Tiffany told me afterwards that she found the presentation so straightforward that she couldn't understand why she'd ever thought it was a problem. The fascinating thing about it was that we'd never discussed her "meeting-anxiety problem." She'd never

mentioned it to me, and she wasn't thinking about it or focusing on it as we talked about innate thinking. She had an insight – a rise in her level of understanding – and her innate clarity, resilience and well-being took care of the rest. It acted where it was needed.

As you'll see, one of the things that connects the stories in this chapter is that the results and benefits each of these people experienced actually showed up when they were looking in a different direction. They weren't "working on" the things that got transformed when their consciousness rose; instead, they were oriented towards deepening their understanding of how life works…

DISTINCTION: Achievement-obsession vs. Understanding-orientation

If a person thinks they live in an outside-in world, it's logical for them to be **achievement-obsessed**. After all – if they believe their happiness, security and well-being comes from (or is threatened by) their external circumstances, then it makes sense for them to focus tirelessly on achieving goals and eliminating problems; turning themselves into a better "achievement machine" by developing their strengths and eliminating weaknesses. When a person is obsessed with achievement, they spend a lot of time in "the known" (you can tell when someone has an **achievement-obsession**, because they often feel stressed and under pressure, and have a greater than average number of relationship difficulties).

Once a person has even an inkling that we live in an inside-out world, it makes sense to adopt an **understanding-orientation**. When a person is oriented towards understanding, they're puzzled and curious about life. They spend more time in a state of wonder, in "the unknown" (the source of creativity and innovation). When you have an **understanding-orientation**, you're looking for a more philosophical perspective on life; an increase in your clarity of understanding. You may very well have goals, dreams and aspirations but you're coming from a different place. You allow wisdom and intuition to guide you as you find opportunities

to develop your strengths. You see the bigger picture, and are more patient and accepting of yourself as you let go of your weaknesses.

Of course, people with an **achievement-obsession** sometimes get an increase in their level of understanding, just as people with an **understanding-orientation** often experience significant improvements in the results they get in life. They're not mutually exclusive. But because the **understanding-orientation** is aiming for a closer alignment with the way life actually works, it offers benefits that aren't usually available to the **achievement-obsessed** individual.

Here's a way of thinking about it. Imagine two doctors living in London in the 1850s. Doctor A believes that illness and disease are caused by bad smells. He spends every available hour on a scheme to supply highly-scented flowers to every hospital ward in the city. He's totally focused on this **achievement**, because he wants the best for his patients. Doctor B is looking in a different direction. He's heard suggestions that illness and disease *aren't* caused by bad smells, but rather by tiny invisible creatures called germs and bacteria. He spends his time exploring this new **understanding,** because he wants the best for his patients.

Paradoxically, when you start to shift to an understanding orientation, it often "raises the bar" on what you're able to achieve. This is something I've seen in my own life (e.g. in the writing of this book), and in the lives of my clients: many of your biggest achievements come *after* you let go of an achievement-obsession, and start increasing your clarity of understanding.

This is one of the biggest differences between traditional application models and the implication model described by Innate Thinking® (as we discussed in Chapter 8). With an application model, a person or organization chooses the goals they want to achieve and the problems they want to resolve, then they work on making those changes (sometimes with the help of a change-worker such as a consultant, facilitator, coach or trainer).

The changes are "achievements," and the success of the application is measured by the degree to which they are achieved. *"So far, so good"* you may be thinking, but think again… If an unhappy person

believes *"I'll be happy when I get into a relationship"* (for instance), the "achievement" of a relationship may, at first glance, look like a big success. But the process of achieving it can actually *reinforce* the outside-in misunderstanding. Now the person thinks they're reliant on the relationship (and their partner) for their security and well-being. This dependence can also foster the background anxiety that the partner might leave, taking their security and well-being with them.

The *Innate Thinking*® model looks in a different direction. A person or organization will still have goals they want to achieve and problems they want to solve, but their attention is turned towards a more accurate understanding of life. All too often, the things people perceive as problems and issues, wants and needs are merely a reflection of their superstitious thinking in the first place. An increase in your clarity of understanding can radically transform the way you relate to what you had been perceiving as important. You may start to notice yourself becoming more accepting of your weaknesses and imperfections, while finding healthy ways to mitigate them.

Case Study: Taking the pressure off

Kevin came from a high-pressure corporate background, where he felt he had to strive for the same things his colleagues wanted (flash cars, expensive suits, champagne, luxury watches etc.). When he started exploring *Innate Thinking*®, Kevin had some powerful increases in understanding, and his whole landscape changed. He discovered that it's OK for him to be himself. Previously he'd been uncomfortable with the thought of living abroad, but he's spent the past few months living in Central Europe. He's not wasting his energy; instead, he's taking the time to live life in a way that feels authentic and true to him. He says that he's experiencing a real sense of purpose, but without any sense of pressure. Kevin now gets huge enjoyment from the simpler things in life; his work as an internet marketer leaves him plenty of time to explore his new surroundings and meet new people. Kevin's clarity of understanding isn't just giving him more happiness and well-being in his life; it's also helping him to follow his wisdom, and do things in ways that work for him. It's going to where it's needed.

Paradoxically, the things people have been perceiving as "problems" diminish in intensity or disappear. Mountains get turned back into molehills, and people find that they have the resources to tackle the things that *do* need dealing with, guided by their innate wisdom.

The achievement-obsession is about optimizing results and solving problems at your existing level of consciousness. The understanding-orientation is about experiencing a *rise* in your level of consciousness. While the rise often results in significant achievements and other benefits, they are side-effects; positive by-products of the deeper understanding.

Case Study: Looking for the formula

Bec was brought to one of my events by a friend. She told me later that, during the event, she had a nice feeling and thought the subject matter was interesting, but wasn't aware of any huge insights. In the weeks that followed, however, it was a different story. Up until then, Bec had been approaching her business in a formulaic way, but that no longer felt right for her. She stopped looking outside herself for "the right way" to do things, and got more connected with her innate wisdom. She told me that it was like being introduced to a "her" that had been hidden away for a long time; a Bec that *knows* she's going to be OK no matter what.

She says *"My life has moved from being rigid and conventional to a place where I'm willing to play with the unknown, and allow for some amazing new possibilities."* While she still gets hoodwinked by her thinking from time to time, she's realizing more and more quickly that it's just that; thinking. Bec explains, *"When this happens, I sit down, slow down, and wait for clarity. And it comes, it always comes."* And the difference isn't just showing up in her own life; it's impacting the way she relates to other people; her children, her clients, her partner. Her formulaic "problem" wasn't something that she'd been looking to solve, but it was causing her unnecessary stress and pressure, so her wisdom gave her what she needed.

Once again: one of the dangers of the achievement-obsession is that the process of achieving from that mindset can reinforce the outside-in misunderstanding; the misperception that our THOUGHT-generated

experiential reality is an actual, material reality, and that our clarity, security and well-being is in some way dependent on it.

Reality Check

Am I saying there's anything wrong with wanting to achieve things? No, I'm not! But there's a huge difference between achievement that's driven by the sense of need and lack (the *"I'll be happy when"* of superstitious thinking) and the achievement that comes as a natural expression of following your wisdom, secure in the knowledge that you are already enough.

The morphine of self-improvement

Outside my window stands a strong, healthy tree, about forty feet tall. Many years ago, a seed was planted in the ground, and it started growing. The roots reach down into the nourishing soil, creating a strong foundation; the leaves absorb sunlight and carbon dioxide, transforming them into life-giving nutrients; the branches and leaves drink in the falling rain. The tree continues growing.

The tree doesn't "work on" growing. It just grows. Growing is its nature.

There's a way in which our attempts to "take control" of our personal evolution can actually interfere with our natural propensity to grow. The seeker's habitual searching is the very thing that stands in the way of them finding what they yearn for. Like an opiate, the intoxicating patterns of struggle and striving numb their emotional pain, while blinding them to the natural joy of living.

"There's nothing in this world that you can't turn into heroin..."

But, like the tree in my garden, it is your nature to grow. Clarity of understanding unlocks the self-love, gratitude and acceptance that are the sunlight, rainwater and nutrients of your personal evolution. While you don't get to decide the timescale, increases in consciousness and clarity of understanding are inevitable for you when you get out of your own way, let your wisdom guide you and start enjoying your life as it is today.

While an understanding-orientation is a natural state of being for a toddler, and would certainly seem rational to a first-year philosophy student, it might seem like a counterintuitive choice for someone living in the "real world" of work, families, goals, businesses, mortgages, health and relationships. But as you follow your wisdom and keep increasing your understanding of innate thinking, you're going to be guided in living a life you love, no matter what.

So what do you need to do in order for that to happen?

---

keep exploring ⁜ connect with others
share your discoveries ⁜ deepen your understanding

Reflection point: Implicit in the idea of "self-improvement" is the assumption that a) there's this thing called a "self," b) it needs to be worked on and improved, and c) the one most qualified to specify and carry out the work is… the self itself! Huh?! Doesn't that seem just a little crazy-making? What would happen if you decided not to treat yourself as a "thing" to be improved, and instead open to the possibility that it's your nature to continue learning, growing and evolving?

There's an entire industry built on the assumption that it's a good idea to relate to yourself as a thing to be improved and worked on. Lots of people will be happy to tell you that makes sense. And while it's fine to take dancing lessons, or learn another language, you cross the line when you start pretending that your "self" needs improving. This one's worth reflecting on for a while. When you're ready, just scan the QR code or type the URL into your browser to get free Chapter 18 resources and shareable digital goodness. Of course, some of the most delectable morsels of goodness are your own insights, so please take a moment to post them for the benefit of the other people who are exploring this chapter…

www.ClarityBook.biz/chapter18

19

Do Nothing

"The Master doesn't try to be powerful;
thus he is truly powerful.
The ordinary man keeps reaching for power;
thus he never has enough.
The Master does nothing,
yet he leaves nothing undone.
The ordinary man is always doing things,
yet many more are left to be done."

Lao Tse, Philosopher

"Point yourself in the right direction and do nothing..."

This provocative statement seemed to fly in the face of everything I "knew" about how to live an inspiring, successful life. It raised questions...

- What's the "right" direction, and how do you know when you're pointed in that direction?
- If you're "doing nothing," how does anything ever get done?
- How is this helpful?

While it was easy for the thrash-metal band of my habitual thinking to raise objections to this statement, I could also feel a truth in it. After all, I was a master of "doing"; I'd accomplished a lot in my life by taking action, but a lot of my "doing" had me running on the hamster wheel of *"I'll be happy when..."* thinking.

My explorations had introduced me to the curious notion of "not-doing." The idea of a more effortless approach to life was certainly appealing to me, but the idea of pointing myself in the right direction and "doing nothing" still sounded like a recipe for inertia, passivity and, ultimately, disaster; particularly in today's fast-moving, fast-changing business environment.

But it turns out that just because you're "doing nothing" doesn't mean that nothing gets done...

DISTINCTION: Misguided action vs. Inspired action

When a person takes action from an outside-in misunderstanding of reality, they're often acting from the superstition that I call "the hidden hamster wheel"; the misguided belief that the action they're taking will lead to results which either give them the felt experience they desire, or stop them from experiencing the feelings which they want to avoid. This superstition is often accompanied by feelings of craving or lack.

I call this superstition-driven action **misguided action**, because it's the result of someone being caught in the outside-in misunderstanding. **Misguided action** is often tinged with striving, urgency and desperation.

On the other hand, when a person takes action from the clarity of the inside-out understanding, they're seeing and feeling the reality of life more clearly. They know (at least intuitively in that moment) that their felt experience can't be threatened by (or delivered by) anything other than their thinking. Acting from this clarity is the essence of high-performance, what athletes, dancers and musicians sometimes refer to as being "in the zone."

When a person acts from clarity, I call it **inspired action**, because it's guided by wisdom and intuition. When people say things like "I felt a sense of calm, and suddenly I just knew exactly what to do," what follows is typically **inspired action**.

Misguided action is when people act on their superstitious thinking, and the feelings of stress and urgency that so often accompany it.

When a person is acting from clarity, they'll still have powerful intuitions about the importance of timing, but there's rarely a feeling of stressful urgency. That's one of the reasons **inspired action** can be so effective and impactful.

"Point yourself in the right direction and do nothing..."

So what are the answers to the questions raised by this curious statement?

1. What's the "right" direction, and how do you know when you're pointed in that direction?

Pointing yourself in the right direction means looking towards what's creating your experience of life; looking to the *source* of your thinking rather than the *products* of your thinking.

And what's creating your experience of life? The principles of innate thinking.

When we're caught up in superstitious thinking, we're fixated on the form of life. Our thinking always looks real, so it appears as if we're well-advised to be obsessing about the form our thinking is taking. When we're seeing how life really works (inside-out), we move back towards clarity, and are in a better position to be guided by wisdom.

In any moment, we can turn our gaze from the *content* of our experience (the products of THOUGHT) to what's *creating* our experience (the principle of THOUGHT.)

2. If you're "doing nothing," how does anything ever get done?

As I use the term, "doing nothing" isn't about the actions you take so much as it is about the thinking that gives *rise* to your actions.

Most people spend much of their lives taking misguided action; "doing" from a superstition-driven mindset and the feelings of stress and urgency that often come with it. When you're "doing nothing," your actions are sponsored by clarity and understanding.

So does that mean you should only take action when you're seeing clearly? Definitely not.

Stay in the game

Woody Allen famously said that 80% of success is showing up. While it's great to feel intrinsically motivated, take inspired action and get into the zone, it's surprising how often the inspiration waits until you're already in the game before it shows up.

My dear friend and colleague, *Stillpower* author Garret Kramer, works with senior executives and professional athletes to help them improve performance and get the results they desire. Neither group has the luxury of sitting around waiting for inspiration to strike – they need to show up, ready to work when their team needs them. Whether they're seeing things clearly or lost in superstitious thinking, Garret's advice is the same; stay in the game!

And why stay in the game? Because, as I said in Chapter 4, the mind is context-sensitive. *Innate Thinking*® points to an extraordinary "intelligence" capable of giving you what you need when you need it. When you stay in the game, and leave your mind to self-correct, your head will clear, and you'll be given what you need to deliver the goods. This is in stark contrast to the person who sits on the sidelines (literally or metaphorically), trying to *"get their head right,"* waiting until they *"feel ready."* I know people who have been waiting for so long to *"feel ready"* that they've become experts at waiting (not a promising field of expertise).

When I got the invitation to appear live on national TV, my superstitious thinking had me squirming and looking for a way out of it. Fortunately, I understood what was happening, so I stayed in the game and showed up. It's the same in everyone's life. When we follow the dubious advice of our insecure, outside-in thinking, we're stuck in "groundhog day," repeating the habits of the past and re-creating what we no longer want.

When we're willing to show up, despite our insecurities, we create new possibilities.

While inspired action feels great, sometimes you just need to do what you think is right, in spite of your superstitious thinking. As you continue allowing yourself to become more responsive to your wisdom, you'll often find that the answers you need come at the exact moment you need them.

Sometimes the "right thing to do" is to take a specific action.

Sometimes the "right thing to do" is to stop and take a rest.

Sometimes the "right thing to do" is to wait for further guidance.

In the meantime, stay in the game!

Inspired marketing

A few years ago, my business scheduled a programme with a great trainer, but our promotions for the event didn't hit the mark, and were met with a lukewarm response. We decided to go ahead with it (a number of people had booked on the event), but we had a problem: we wanted it to be a great experience for everyone, and the group size was smaller than we wanted it to be.

We brainstormed an approach that we thought *might* help us fill the programme. We weren't particularly hopeful about the results it would get, but we felt like we had to do something! I went away with a list of actions. Then something amazing happened…

I didn't do *any* of the things on the list. I procrastinated, saying "I'll do it tomorrow," and not taking action. Meanwhile, the start of the event drew ever nearer.

Another dear friend and colleague, *Supercoach* author Michael Neill, once told me he's amazed at how often what *looks* like procrastination turns out to be his wisdom. I reflected on this as I continued doing nothing on the marketing…

Then, with just a few weeks to go before the programme started, I had a sudden flash of insight. I saw how I could offer the programme to a group of my most loyal clients in a way that would be hard to say "no" to. I intuitively knew it was the right thing to do. It took 20 minutes, very little effort, and had a response three or four times better than what we'd anticipated from the approach we'd brainstormed. The programme filled up and the event was a big success.

People love closure, the feeling of "knowing" and being right. But, if we're willing to spend some time "not knowing" and looking to our wisdom, the results are often remarkable. If you're willing to wait, your wisdom will often provide an answer very quickly. At other times it may take longer, but the more you're willing to "not know," the more you'll realize how many things aren't actually as urgent as we sometimes pretend.

But what about those times when you need to make a decision immediately, and you're not getting a clear steer from your wisdom one way or another? In those situations, you make the best decision you can based on the information available. These are exactly the moments when the best thing you've got going for you is clarity. When all other factors are equal, the person with the clearest head is holding the strongest hand.

3. How is this helpful?

In Chapter 9, I explained that your understanding of how life works has more influence than any other factor over our experience of life, and the results we get. This is particularly important when it comes to the actions we take, because...

Every action a person takes is consistent with their understanding of how life works (even if they can't explain why that's so):

- the CEO works an 80-hour week because it makes sense to them

- the athlete trains hard because it makes sense to them

- the alcoholic drinks because it makes sense to them

- the manager checks their email every ten minutes because it makes sense to them

- the devout worshipper attends church because it makes sense to them

- the surgeon masters their craft because it makes sense to them

- the criminal robs a bank because it makes sense to them

- the student stays up late studying for their exam because it makes sense to them

- the OCD-sufferer washes their hands for the fiftieth time that day because it makes sense to them

- etc., etc., etc....

The actions we take are informed by our understanding of how life works, and serve to reinforce that understanding. When we act from the outside-in misunderstanding, the actions we take reinforce that (mis)understanding. When we act from an inside-out understanding of life, the actions we take *endorse* that understanding. *Even if it's the same action!*

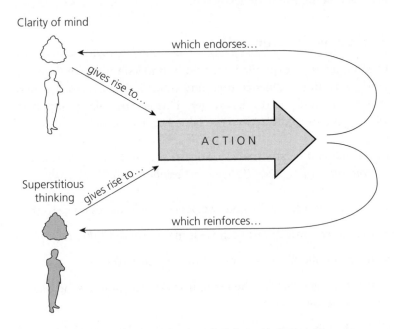

Figure 19.1 Actions Endorse/Reinforce Understanding

Of course, over time, the cumulative results of living and acting from a certain understanding of life (and the feeling-states it engenders) can start to mount up...

- People who worry a lot find no shortage of things to worry about.

- People who are easily satisfied tend to be contented and enjoy what they have.

- People who think there's somewhere to get to and that "there" is better than "here" don't tend to spend much time enjoying the present moment.

- People without much on their mind tend to have a rich experience of life.

- A person who consistently acts from superstitious thinking will tend to have an experience of life that reflects their lack of understanding.

- A person who consistently acts from clarity, guided by wisdom and an inside-out understanding will tend to have an experience of life that reflects their clarity of understanding.

Reality Check

But if the actions a person takes reinforce their understanding of how life works, doesn't that mean that people *will* "be happy when" they get the things they *think* will make them happy? Sadly not. The actions reinforce their understanding, but life only works one way: inside-out. What typically happens to people on the hidden hamster wheel is that they either:

a) *prevent themselves from getting what they want, or*

b) *get what they want, experience a temporary high, then feel deflated, going "I guess that wasn't it after all – now I need to figure out what I really want."*

In both these cases, the *"I'll be happy when…"* superstition stays intact.

So, when you're staying in the game, leaving your thinking to self-correct and increasing your clarity of understanding, a world of new possibilities starts opening up for you. Your increasing enjoyment in leading your own life may even inspire you to start guiding others in this direction. Either way, it's worth getting the inside track on...

keep exploring ❖ connect with others
share your discoveries ❖ deepen your understanding

Reflection point: How would your life be different moving forward if you were willing to show up and stay in the game, regardless of any superstitious thinking you may have? What are some of the things you might find yourself doing? What are some of the new possibilities you might notice opening up to you? What are some of the ways you might find yourself enjoying a richer, more fulfilling experience of life?

By the way, if you've been thinking of sharing your insights but were feeling insecure about it, this is a great opportunity to get in the game. Just scan the QR code or type the URL into your browser, then experiment with sharing your comments. You'll find some great extra resources relating to Chapter 19, and who *knows* what other possibilities you'll be opening up…

www.ClarityBook.biz/chapter19

20

The Leadership Delusion

....

"Leaders don't create followers, they create more leaders."

Ralph Nader, Attorney
consumer advocate,
and political activist

"Here's the problem: Our business is growing steadily at 25%. We're taking on new staff every year, but we haven't found a way to develop new leaders at anything like the same rate..."

I was speaking with the practice manager for a consulting group that works with Global 1000 companies. His comments echo a sentiment I've heard repeatedly from company directors over the years, *"We need more leaders; they're hard to find and even harder to make!"*

If you google the phrase "10 keys to leadership success" (or similar), you'll be presented with a plethora of articles. The "keys" they offer are many and varied: some show up again and again, over a number of articles (*focus, have a vision, be a team-builder*), others less so (*collaborate, contribute*). Some seem blindingly obvious (*make great decisions, communicate, be coherent*) while others come with a double-helping of "Mom and apple pie" (*care, be honest, keep your integrity*). A recent search for the term "leadership" on Amazon returned 65,975 books. All over the world, people attend programmes, read books and listen to audios, trying to master the skills and qualities of leadership. Companies send people on numerous types of team-building programmes in the hopes of "revealing" their employees' leadership qualities. If the number of books in print is anything to go by, our hunger for "leadership skills" is enormous and growing. But here's the thing:

If the 65,975 books were looking in the right direction, don't you think we would have found the solution to "the leadership problem" by now?

DISTINCTION: Symptoms vs. Causes

In the Introduction, I introduced the metaphor of a cold, explaining that *acting like* you have the **symptoms** of a cold is difficult and unconvincing. But when you *have* a cold, the bug **causes** the symptoms to emerge effortlessly and authentically.

Most leadership books and programmes make a valiant effort to help people master the **symptoms** of leadership; behaviours, skills and attitudes, modelled from successful leaders (some of them *extremely* successful).

Unfortunately, *acting like* you have the **symptoms** of leadership is difficult and unconvincing, because the **symptoms** aren't what's doing the "heavy-lifting." But when you have the "leadership bug," it **causes** the symptoms to emerge effortlessly and authentically. The real power-source is the **cause** that gives rise to the symptoms.

An innate capacity for leadership

I was working with a group recently, and we were exploring the subject of leadership. I explained the "symptoms/causes" distinction, then invited the group to make a list of what they considered the causes of leadership to be. Here are some of the "causes" they came up with:

- Vision
- Passion
- Goals
- Contribution
- Flexibility
- Listening
- Being decisive
- Stillness
- Action
- Teambuilding

When we got to 10 causes, I said *"Congratulations – you now have the content to write the next '10 keys to leadership success' article."* I explained that, while the items they'd identified were certainly valuable, they were actually symptoms or "effects" of the leadership bug, rather than the causes.

So what causes leadership? What's the "bug" that gives rise to these symptoms? And how does a person catch it? I've got some good news, some bad news and some great news:

- **Good news:** you've already got it; everyone has the "cause" of leadership within them.

- **Bad news:** for most people it's covered over, shrouded in layers of superstitious thinking.

- **Great news:** fortunately, superstitious thinking is an illusion; as you increase your clarity of understanding, and continue seeing through the illusion, you awaken your innate capacity for leadership.

Highway mirage

Sometimes, when you're driving on a hot day, you see a mirage on the road ahead; an optical illusion that looks like a pool of water. The first time you see one, it's a little strange, but you quickly learn that there's no pool of water in the road. It's just a mirage – an illusion – so you don't need to take any evasive action.

Superstitious thinking is like a mirage. Like the flat earth, the geo-centric universe, and the miasma theory of disease, it's an illusion that has no grounding in reality. All superstitious thinking is based on a misunderstanding about life, the mistaken belief that we can feel something *other than* our thinking in the moment. That belief is 100% false; it doesn't work that way.

And, like a mirage, superstitious thinking is just an illusion,
so you don't need to take any evasive action when you notice it.
Understanding its nature is enough.

As we explored in Chapter 4, clarity, inner security and peace of mind are the default setting for people; our natural state when our minds are clear and uncluttered with superstitious thinking. The "deep drivers" described in Chapter 4 are the expressions of your innate capacity for leadership; an emergent property of innate thinking. As you begin to see past your superstitious thinking, the deep drivers shine through, and the "symptoms" of leadership start showing up. This is also what's going on when people say that a person has "character."

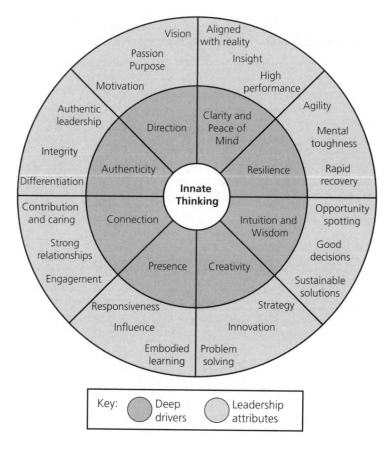

Figure 20.1 Innate Thinking Drives Leadership Attributes

Take a moment to contrast some of the attributes of clarity with those of superstitious thinking (see overleaf).

Feel free to add your own distinctions to this list. The fact is, when we're lost in superstitious thinking, we can't help but show up on the left side of the list. But the moment we realize that it's just a mirage, we're on our way back to the right side.

Attributes of superstitious thinking	Attributes of clarity
Clouded, repetitive, clogged	Clear, fresh, free-flowing
Unresponsive, stuck in the past	Responsive, present, in the moment
Change-averse, inflexible, rigid	Agile, flexible, open to change
Serious, insecure, boring	Playful, confident, fun
Tense, preoccupied, struggling to learn	Relaxed, alert, learns quickly and easily
Traumatized, weak, helpless	Resilient, tough, persistent
False, fake, defended, closed	Authentic, real, transparent, open, unique
Flat, dull, repetitive, unmotivated, passive	Passionate, inspired, purposeful, motivated, proactive
Fearful, anxious, worried	Fearless, curious, experimental
Isolated, separate, lonely, shut down	Connected, warm, listening, loving
Self-centred, harsh, cruel	Understanding, kind, compassionate
Stressed, taking things personally	Peace of mind, philosophical, reflective
Dissatisfied, sense of lack, needy, greedy	Appreciative, grateful, contented, giving
Reactive, habitual, indecisive	Intuitive, guided by wisdom, decisive
Stale, habitual, closed	Creative, innovative, open to new ideas
Follower, bureaucrat, consumer	Leader, entrepreneur, creator

If only I knew how...

One of the most common laments I hear from people is this:

"I'd follow my dreams and do what I want to do, but I don't know how."

This looks like a reality to the people who say it, but it's 100% superstitious thinking. Despite the sale of millions of copies of *"How to..."* books and programmes each year, very few people take action and put what they learn into practice. Here's why. The *"How to..."* book has usually been written by someone who accomplished something of value. They then capture the steps they took to accomplish it in a book, training course, or multimedia programme. Innocently, they're sharing the *symptoms* of their accomplishment, but not the *causes*. If the symptoms are like apples, the causes are the tree that grew them. When people buy *"How to"* books and programmes, they're unknowingly trying to glue someone else's apples onto their tree, without realizing an essential fact: it doesn't work that way! Think about it. Someone who's accomplished something of value and written a *"How to..."* book has likely had to do a number of essential things:

- They've taken responsibility for themselves and their results.
- They've clarified their sense of direction, and found their authentic voice.
- They've stepped into the spotlight, and risked criticism and/or failure.
- They've looked within themselves for security, resilience and persistence.
- They've honed their intuition, and strengthened their decision-making-muscles.
- They've developed their creative process, and discovered the "how-tos" that fit for them.

These are some of the key elements of leadership. But the "how to" book can't give you these; you have to grow your own. When you look to someone else to tell you how to do what's right for you, you're accidentally giving your power away, implying that they know and you don't. Programmes that teach the "how tos" of leadership without an understanding of the underlying causes are subtly reinforcing the follower mindset. Which begs a question:

If leaders are supposed to create more leaders,
shouldn't leadership programmes stop creating more followers?

Why is it like this?

A compliant workforce

The Industrial Revolution created a huge need for a compliant workforce to man the factories, but there was a problem. Most of the workers were accustomed to seasonal work relating to farming and crop cycles. The regimented timetable of factory life was foreign to them, and when they had amassed enough money to pay for a few days' worth of food and drink, many of them would stop coming to work.

This caused a huge problem for the factory owners, who needed consistency of production. So they exerted pressure for the introduction of mandatory schooling, and gave generous donations to the clergy, whose sermons started including messages about the nobility of labour, the importance of obedience and "an honest day's work for an honest day's pay." The school system was designed along factory lines to create good workers; consistent, obedient, conditioned.

It didn't have much effect on the first generation of factory workers. It was only when their *children* arrived for work that the strategy played out. For over 200 years, the majority of people have internalized huge amounts of superstitious thinking telling them that there's a right way of doing things, that they don't know what it is, and that someone in authority needs to tell them the answer. As a result, many (most?) people have become dependent on others to tell them what to do in at least *some* important aspects of their lives.

Arguably, this kind of conditioning was necessary for our stage of development in the 1800s, but it's way past its sell-by date today. The challenges being faced by modern businesses require all the clarity, creativity, and agility we can muster. We need leaders who are willing to take responsibility, decisions, risks and action.

Thought Experiment

Stop for a moment, and have a guess at how much of your working life has been spent lost in superstitious thinking. Now have a guess at how much of your colleagues' working lives have been spent lost in it. Now have a guess at the number of unnecessary conflicts, missed deadlines and botched jobs have come from all that superstitious thinking. Now have a guess at all the sick days and stress-induced illnesses that have resulted from it. Now multiply it by all the businesses in the country; in the world.

To an individual, to a business, to the entire economy; the cost of superstitious thinking is astronomical, not just in terms of lost productivity and unnecessary problems, but in terms of squandered energy, unused creativity and missed opportunities.

Organizational corruption, deception and breaches of integrity (e.g. The Enron collapse, the Barclays Libor scandal and the Goldman Sachs affair) are all the result of superstitious, outside-in thinking (in the form of fear, greed and selfishness).

Fortunately, as you continue increasing your understanding of *Innate Thinking®*, you'll find your innate leadership capacities emerging and developing. This creates a strong platform for you to lead from, to create from and to learn from. You see, as you develop your leadership capacities, you can learn from any person, book or programme. You intuitively know what's right for you, taking what fits and leaving what doesn't. And this doesn't just apply to leadership...

Beating the bell curve

Here are some of the more popular "soft skills" courses that companies and individuals invest in:

Leadership skills	Personal development	HR management
Management skills	Sales and marketing	Change management
Coaching skills	Conflict resolution	Time management
Negotiation skills	Goal setting	Project management
Presentation skills	Personality typing	Stress management
Influence skills	Customer engagement	Anger management
Communication skills	Employee engagement	Team management

Unfortunately, every company (and every trainer) knows that there's a bell curve of response to any training programme. For a given course, some people will be deeply impacted, demonstrating genuine change, with new attitudes, skills and behaviours. Others will experience little or no impact, showing no evidence of any learning having taken place. The rest will be distributed across the curve, with most people being somewhere in the middle.

Clarity is the unrecognized factor that determines where on the bell curve you show up...

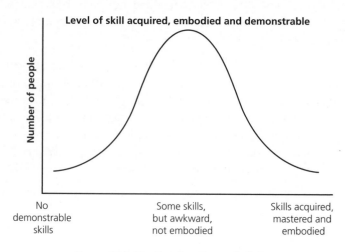

Figure 20.2 The Training Course Bell Curve

DISTINCTION: Information vs. Implementation

It's never been easier to find high-quality **information** about how to accomplish whatever you want to accomplish. Yet it's surprising how often people struggle with **implementation**, even when they're armed with first class tactics and a step-by-step action plan. That's because, while the intellect can *always* make room for some tantalizing new **information**, it's unlikely to be **implemented** until it fits with the person's understanding of how life works. An update to your understanding relies on an insight.

Implementation typically involves the "4Ts"; taking responsibility, taking decisions, taking risks and taking action. These can often bring up superstitious thinking. When you can see through the mirage of that thinking, **implementation** is relatively straightforward. When you can't see through it, more **information** can look like an attractive proposition.

As you keep having insights, and increasing your clarity of understanding, you may be surprised at how much more **implementation**-oriented you find yourself being.

While some of this can be explained away by the fact that some people arrive with a "natural aptitude" towards a given skillset, that's only part of the story. The more important part of the story resides in the fact that a person's clarity of mind has a huge impact on their ability to learn, and on their performance in the moment.

The biggest leverage point for any "soft skill" is
your understanding of innate thinking...

Traditional approaches to coaching, training and organizational change are grounded in *application-based learning*; teaching techniques, skills and methods, then encouraging people to implement them. While these approaches can be useful for routine mechanical processes, their effectiveness drops off sharply for complex cognitive and creative skill-sets. Why?

Because successful implementation depends on clarity, and the qualities it brings.

The *Innate Thinking*® model is grounded in *Implication-based Learning*™, focusing on the foundational principles that drive high-performance. With this approach, there is no separate implementation step. As individuals see the *implications* of these foundational principles, *implementation* is automatic.

Of course, this doesn't just apply to selling; it applies to *all* soft skills. Clarity of mind isn't just the ideal platform to *learn* from; it's also the ideal platform to *lead* from. Once again:

> *When you've got nothing on your mind,*
> *you're free to give your best.*

The secret of successful selling

Every successful salesperson knows that the single most influential factor in closing a deal is the *client's* experience during the sales process. And what's the biggest factor that influence's the client's experience? The experience the *salesperson* is having.

If the salesperson has clarity of mind, they'll connect easily with the client, listen deeply, and respond intuitively and effectively. They'll feel secure in themselves, and have a service-orientation, looking for the solution that's best for the client. The client will usually "pick up" on the salesperson's felt experience, and will bring their own clarity and comfort to the decision-making process.

But all too often, salespeople *don't* have clarity of mind; instead, their heads are clogged with superstitious thinking. They're worried about hitting their sales targets, or trying to remember what the next step of their company's sales process is. They're focused on making the client like them, and afraid of feeling rejected. As a result, they come across as needy and desperate.

The solution to this is simple: clarity of understanding. When you have an insightful understanding of innate thinking, you know clarity of

---

mind is your strongest card. When your head fills up with superstitious thinking (as it does for all of us from time to time), you notice and allow it to self-correct. You unconsciously telegraph your sense of security, comfort and wisdom to your client, as you support them in making the decision that's genuinely right for them.

While there's certainly a place for skills training – I wouldn't want to be operated on by a surgeon who hadn't been to medical school – it's only part of the puzzle. I also wouldn't want to be operated on by a surgeon who had a head full of superstitious thinking about her marriage, her mortgage or her surgical skills!

So what is the leadership delusion? The misguided belief that a person can find the source of leadership outside themselves.

The true source of leadership resides in clarity of mind
and clarity of understanding,
giving you what you need in the moment
to deal with the matter at hand.

While there are certainly skills to be developed and mastered, they needed to be grounded in the "inner" qualities of leadership. And the fastest way to develop those is by increasing your clarity of understanding.

An insight into the principles of innate thinking is an increase in your clarity of understanding; a more practical relationship to how your mind works. As your clarity of understanding increases, you'll experience the "symptoms" of that increase (the attributes of clarity). Because the symptoms are more "visible" than the cause, it's natural that we get seduced by the idea of working on the symptoms; looking in the direction of the attributes *("the light's better here...")*. But it makes far more sense to nurture the cause.

You can nurture the cause by continuing
to increase your understanding of innate thinking.

And that means that something wonderful is possible for you…

**keep exploring ⁙ connect with others
share your discoveries ⁙ deepen your understanding**

Reflection point: What's it like for you to recognize that you have the source of the greatest leadership capacities already right there within you? You can "activate" them more and more fully by deepening your understanding of innate thinking.

Isn't that good to know? Now take the lead; scan the QR code or type the URL into your browser when you're ready to step up and start sharing your discoveries. You'll also find additional resources you can explore to continue increasing your clarity of understanding…

www.ClarityBook.biz/chapter20

21

Living a Life You Love

....

*"We must be willing to get rid
of the life we've planned,
so as to have the life that is waiting for us.
The old skin has to be shed
before the new one can come."*

Joseph Campbell, Mythologist,
writer and lecturer

"Now let me ask you something I think we all know the answer to: the test is rigged, isn't it? You programmed it to be unwinnable..."

In a pivotal scene from the 2009 film, *Star Trek*, a young James T Kirk (played by Chris Pine) is defending himself against the charge of cheating on the Kobayashi Maru test (a highly realistic battle simulation designed to gauge the trainee's response to a no-win scenario). Kirk is the first person ever to beat the test, but Spock (the test's designer) has accused him of breaking the rules. Kirk's defence is that *the test itself* is a cheat; that if a game has been designed to be unwinnable, you don't have to play by the rules of the game.

So how is this relevant?

Here's how: the outside-in misunderstanding turns life into an unwinnable game. The *"I'll be happy when..."* and *"I couldn't be happy if..."* superstitions promise us that happiness, security and well-being are waiting for us "out there" in the distance or in the future. Whether it's five years, five miles or five seconds away, the outside-in misunderstanding tells us that our heart's desire is just out of reach, just out there at the end of our thinking. But it's not true and it never has been. That's not how it works.

When we look to the outside world for our happiness, security and peace of mind, we're looking in the wrong direction. It doesn't matter whether it's the "there" of material possessions or personal accomplishments, self-improvement or spirituality. The moment we think there's somewhere to get to, and that "there" is better than "here," we've stepped out of our sanity and into an unwinnable game.

So what does it mean to step out of the unwinnable game, and back into our sanity? What does it mean to live a life you love, regardless of its ups and downs?

The search is over

Back in 2004, before I insightfully understood the principles of innate thinking, I used to run a workshop called *The Art of Being*. At the start of the first day, as people began to get comfortable, I would say something like this:

"You know that thing that you've been searching for… your heart's desire? The thing you've been seeking for all these years? I'd like to invite you to open to the possibility that you can have it today… Have it here… Have it now…"

The moment they heard this, people would start shifting uncomfortably in their seats, and I would mimic their internal dialogue, anxiously saying:

"I really do want it… And I'm really looking forward to having it… But today's a bit soon… See, I've got a busy month, and rather a lot on my mind… But I was thinking, a few weeks from now is looking really good… It's what I want most in the world, so I'll definitely make space for it… But if you could just arrange things so it arrives next month… That'll give me time to do what I need to do… Next month will be just perfect…"

Whether you call it the self-image, the ego or superstitious thinking, there's one thing it can't stand: the knowledge that the life you desire is already here; that you don't need anything else to be OK; that you can live a life you love, starting now. Of course, I understood that *intellectually* back in 2004, but I didn't have an embodied understanding of it. So I kept on seeking. Kept on searching. Until one day I realized something for myself…

The search is over.

As you continue deepening your understanding of innate thinking, you'll see that searching and seeking is inconsistent with the knowledge that you already have everything you need within you; that searching and seeking is just another flavour of the unwinnable game. The very feeling we've been interpreting as *"there's something I need to search for"* is, in fact, the feeling of some superstitious thinking, and nothing else. There's nothing missing. You were born whole, and you still are whole.

The moment we stop looking outside ourselves for that which can only be found within, our whole world changes. As your world-view continues shifting from outside-in to inside-out, it's inevitable that you'll love yourself and your life more and more, *whatever* form it takes.

Reality Check

Am I saying that understanding innate thinking will transform the circumstances of a person's life into something wonderful? No. I'm saying that when a person sees life from a greater clarity of understanding, they have a deeper, more profound experience of life, *whatever* their circumstances.

Of course, when a person is living in a richer felt experience, and allowing themselves to be guided by wisdom, the circumstances of their lives often change too, but there's the paradox:

Once you realize your happiness, security and well-being
isn't dependent on your circumstances, it gets easier
to change your circumstances.

A practical example

Two people doing the same kind of work have lost their jobs and are both applying for the same position. Both are equally well-qualified for the new post. The only difference between the two is that one has an embodied understanding of the principles behind innate thinking and the other doesn't. When they go to the job interview, the contrast is huge. One is clear-headed, relaxed and alert, while the other is feeling anxious and insecure. One listens deeply to the interviewer, and starts feeling connected to them, while the other feels self-conscious and isolated. One is in touch with their wisdom and creativity, while the other has a congested, speedy mind. Who do you think is more likely to get the job? The person who feels peaceful, present and secure in themselves? Or the one who's feeling anxious, insecure and needy? It's a no-brainer.

Life seems to respond in a similar way. When you are living from clarity, being guided by wisdom, life is free to unfold gracefully with each step you take. There will still be ups and downs; that's part of being human. But we've evolved to *appreciate* life. Our psychological immune system exists to guide us into a natural, enjoyable experience of life. Our natural response to life is gratitude and appreciation, when there's nothing else in the way. And what gets in the way? Superstitious thinking!

What follows is a list of gentle reminders to help you stay on track, living a life you love. They are not rules or "how tos," but they may serve to spark an insight or an a-ha that makes a difference for you at one time or another.

More importantly, they are not something you need to do, practice, or even remember. Everything you need is already right there within you; there's nothing you need to do to have a life you love.

Appreciation
When you find yourself in a more profound felt experience of life, appreciate it. This isn't a doing – it's more of a not-doing. Our deeper feelings of love, peace and well-being carry valuable information that can correct our thought-system, bringing it into closer connection with reality. So when you notice these feelings arising, allow yourself to stay with them.

Gratitude
Gratitude is like fertilizer for new insights. When you're feeling grateful for what you've already seen, you create fertile soil for new insights to blossom. Conversely, searching and seeking (with the sense of lack they imply) is like soaking the ground in weed-killer. Gratitude and appreciation are natural responses to insight, and to being alive, so you can enjoy them when they come.

Don't try to figure it out
Like the sun behind the clouds, your clarity, security and peace of mind are always within you, whether you're aware of it or not. But you can't *think* your way to clarity and well-being, so there's

no point in trying to figure it out. That just creates more thinking, which is the only thing that's ever blocking your awareness of clarity in the first place. Instead, you can relax, and recognize that everything you're experiencing is a demonstration of innate thinking in action.

Understanding is a rational goal

Everyone likes to feel good, but when we make that our goal, we use all our old habits of thinking to achieve it (with predictable results). When your goal is increasing your clarity of understanding, then every experience is an opportunity to learn; to see how the principles of innate thinking are creating an experience of life in this moment.

Pause when agitated

When you're feeling anxious, insecure and agitated, your thinking looks absolutely real. But we're always feeling our thinking in the moment, and an agitated feeling means agitated thinking; nothing more, nothing less. While I don't recommend you do anything about it – let it change when it changes – your wisdom will remind you that you're in the feeling of your thinking. That's the signal that the system is self-correcting. When that wise thought occurs to you, pay attention, and it will guide you back to clarity.

Look to the source

In any situation, we're either aligned with the outside-in misunderstanding (looking towards the *products* of innate thinking), or with the inside-out reality (looking towards the *principles* behind innate thinking). When we're lost in superstitious thinking, it can seem like the only way of perceiving a situation. But, in any moment, you can look away from the results of your thinking, and towards its source, the principles of MIND, CONSCIOUSNESS and THOUGHT. Once again, this isn't a do-ing, but rather something that happens when you step out of the unwinnable game, and keep waking up to your wisdom.

You don't need to be vigilant

So many people (myself included) have learned to be vigilant with their thinking, trying to monitor and manage their experience. This results in a bunch more thinking, which can block them from the experience of clarity, which is the very thing they were trying to get in the first place. You don't need to do this anymore. When you have an insight, it updates your thought-system. You don't need to work on it.

Be kind to yourself

If being hard on yourself was going to work, it would have worked by now. I encourage you to be kind, gentle and loving with yourself. We all have flaws, frailties and weaknesses; you can love yourself as you are, warts and all. Paradoxically, when we love and accept ourselves as we are, things that used to be utterly resistant to change can suddenly shift effortlessly. Or not. Be kind to yourself, either way. Once again, this isn't really something to do; it's more something to be aware of and open to. As your superstitious thinking continues clearing out, you may start noticing just how much you already love yourself, but just hadn't fully realized it until now. (If that sentence makes you feel uncomfortable, do remember that you're feeling your thinking.)

Lighten up

Oscar Wilde famously said *"Life is too important to be taken seriously."* The *feeling* of seriousness is just a signal that we have serious thinking, but if we don't know that, it can be a grind. While there are situations that require a serious response, there's no need to *feel* serious about it. Love, peace and clarity often carry the information you need to solve the more challenging issues in life, and those deeper feelings are incompatible with the *feeling* of seriousness (though it's still fine to behave seriously when necessary).

Follow your wisdom

Your wisdom will guide you from wherever you are now to your most fulfilling, inspiring life. Wisdom doesn't make us immune to the ups and downs of life, but it helps us to live life in a way that fits perfectly with who we are. As you learn to navigate by wisdom, and deepen your understanding of innate thinking, you'll find yourself living a life you love, more and more each day.

Keep increasing your clarity of understanding

Semmelweis' insight about puerperal fever transformed the world of medicine. Something that's obvious to everyone reading this book was totally invisible to the physicians of 150 years ago. We live in a world that is as lost in the outside-in misunderstanding as the doctors were in the pre-Semmelweis world of miasmas and "atmospheres." When you make it a priority to increase your understanding, you're empowering your shift from the pre-principles, outside-in misunderstanding to the inside-out paradigm. And to living a life you love.

The power of principles revisited

Earlier in the book, I used the metaphor of a football being held underwater to symbolize a person's innate clarity, resilience and well-being. As soon as the hand holding the football releases it, the ball rises to the surface.

The reason the ball rises so reliably is because of buoyancy. When you immerse a floating object in a container of water, the pressure increases the deeper you go due to the weight of the water above. The differences in water pressure exert an upward force on the immersed object, which raises it to the surface. There are precise factors that govern the rate at which an immersed object will rise, including weight, density and friction. But these factors are all governed by a single principle; the principle of gravity. As previously mentioned, a principle is "the fundamental source or basis for something."

Buoyancy works the same way for everyone because gravity doesn't play favourites. It's nothing personal, and there are no exceptions. In the same way, the principles that give rise to our innate clarity, security and well-being work the same way for everyone on the planet. It's not personal, and there are no exceptions.

So, if this is genuinely a "new paradigm," what does that mean for the world of business and work in the years to come? And what does it mean for us as individuals?

keep exploring ⁘ connect with others
share your discoveries ⁘ deepen your understanding

Reflection point: The search is over. You probably realize now that any lingering sense you may have had that there's somewhere to get to (and that there is better than here) is an illusion. There's nowhere to get to. You don't need to improve yourself. The search is over. It's fine to have goals, dreams and aspirations, but <u>you</u> are already fine.

To paraphrase Leonard Cohen, you can stop trying to make yourself into a masterpiece, and relax into the *real* masterpiece. Life is in progress. When you've finished reflecting on this for now, scan the QR code or enter the URL into your browser to get additional resources, share your discoveries and learn from the comments others are posting.

www.ClarityBook.biz/chapter21

22

Capitalizing on Chaos, Complexity and Uncertainty

*"We are at that very point in time
when a 400-year-old age is dying
and another is struggling to be born –
a shifting of culture, science, society and
institutions enormously greater than
the world has ever experienced."*

Dee Ward Hock, Founder
and former CEO of Visa

"Everything that can be invented has been invented..."

A popular myth credits the 1899 commissioner of the US patent office with this quaintly absurd statement. And while there's no *hard* evidence that he actually said it, the last hundred years have been peppered with short-sighted predictions asserting what wouldn't be useful, wouldn't be feasible or wouldn't be possible. All the way from the first telephone to the world wide web, as each technological revolution is on the verge of dawning, someone goes on record to say it's not going to happen. Then it happens.

The world is changing fast. Increases in speed, complexity and knowledge are accompanied by attention-poverty, time-scarcity and information-overwhelm. People shake their heads in the face of chaos, complexity and uncertainty, harking back to simpler times. But what if there's a larger pattern behind the changes we're experiencing?

The waves of transformation

In their seminal book *The Third Wave,* Alvin and Heidi Toffler use the metaphor of waves to describe the revolutionary changes that have swept over the globe through history. Each "wave" solves existing problems, while creating new possibilities, new benefits and new challenges. Solutions to the new problems are delivered by the next wave. In brief, here are the three waves the Tofflers described:

1st wave: The Agricultural Revolution (Domestication)
The 1st wave starts around 8000 BC with the *domestication and farming* of plants and animals, resulting in stabilization of food supplies. Over time, increasing *agricultural wealth* allows farming cultures with *food economies* to dominate hunter-gatherer cultures.

2nd wave: The Industrial Revolution (Mechanization)
The 2nd wave starts around 1760 with the *mechanization* of manual labour, resulting in the mass production of goods. *Industrial wealth* results in *manufacturing economies* that dominate agricultural societies.

> *3rd wave: The Information Revolution (Digitization)*
> The 3rd wave starts around 1940 with the *digitization* of information.
> The *knowledge economy* rewards *informational wealth*, and dominates
> information-poor industrial cultures.

The current wave-shift

There are numerous signals that let us know the 3rd wave (Information Revolution) is continuing to grow and the 2nd wave
(Industrial Revolution) is ebbing. In fact, the attention-poverty,
time-scarcity, information-saturation and connection-starvation
so many people are experiencing is the inevitable consequence
of the outside-in misunderstanding in the context of the current
wave-shift.

> *The uncertainties and complexities we face*
> *are too great to be solved by intellect and analysis alone.*
> *Clarity (with all it entails) is the key to solving the big issues*
> *that face us, and to creating a sustainable future for ourselves,*
> *for our organizations, and for the generations that follow us...*

- We need *clarity*, so we can bring a systemic perspective to solving problems and creating possibilities.

- We need *direction*, so we can create a meaningful and compelling future.

- We need *wisdom*, so we can make wise decisions in the face of
  chaos and complexity.

- We need *connection*, so we can enjoy the richness and sense of
  belonging it brings.

- We need *authenticity*, so we can be true to ourselves, and lead
  with integrity.

- We need *resilience*, so we can negotiate life's many challenges,
  with grace and dignity.

- We need *creativity*, so we can create the sustainable solutions and innovations we require.

- We need *presence*, so we can inspire trust, and stay connected with reality.

As each wave emerges, the culture embraces new stories about its future; new images of itself (remember those 1950s newsreels predicting the robot-enabled, leisure-age of the future?) As the previous wave's future-images start to fade and disintegrate, positive new stories are needed that align with the new wave and nourish the culture with hope for what it promises.

This is one of the key tasks for leaders; to create inspiring and compelling visions of our possible futures.

There are early indicators (and early adopters) as each wave emerges. For instance, computers used to be the domain of scientists, the military and big business. As the 3rd wave gathered power, "computer geeks," hobbyists and other early-adopters got involved. The past 30 years have seen computers move from the specialist fringe to the consumer mainstream as they've become integrated into our daily living.

This last point is essential. There's a close correlation between adoption of emergent wave-drivers (*domestication, mechanization, digitization*) and commercial success. The individuals and companies that embraced the Industrial Revolution prospered. The early-adopters of information technology won a massive advantage over those who hesitated. In fact, the largest and most profitable enterprises are those that fully embrace the emergent wave-drivers (e.g. Apple, Microsoft, Google, Amazon etc.).

We're now in the midst of the Information Revolution – more people than ever before earn their living participating in knowledge work. So what's going to start transforming the knowledge economy?

Early signs of the 4th wave

The "advance signals" of the 4th wave started arriving in the late 19th century with the birth of the field of psychology. The business world was quick to embrace psychology for commercial purposes, using it to influence public opinion, customers and employees alike. Over the past 40 years, the signals have been arriving more and more quickly:

- The rise of the human potential movement, positive psychology and increasing interest in personal development.

- Identification of the need for "emotional intelligence" in the workplace.

- The desire for authenticity, integrity and transparency in the companies we do business with.

- Increasing business focus on identifying and developing the qualities of leadership.

- The decline of many institutions that we previously relied on for a sense of security, purpose and belonging (e.g. religions, education system, postal sevice, civil service, large companies, jobs for life etc.).

- People looking elsewhere for security, belonging and purpose as they pursue "portfolio careers" and move towards greater independence and personal freedom.

Understanding the nature of THOUGHT

The 1st, 2nd and 3rd waves have each been driven by an insightful understanding of the wave's key leverage point:

- 1st wave (Agricultural Revolution): understanding of farming/ agriculture.

- 2nd wave (Industrial Revolution): understanding of mechanization/industry.

- 3rd wave (Information Revolution): understanding of information/digitization/computerization.

The deeper our understanding of the "leverage point" within a given wave, the more power we have to create value.

Most people these days would concede that their thinking has at least *some* part to play in their experience of life. The advance signals of the 4th wave have seen people try to influence their thinking in a variety of ways, using techniques, rituals and methodologies. As people start to see that thinking plays a role in their experience, it's natural that they would try and use it to *influence* that experience. But while people have correctly identified that thinking is an incredibly powerful leverage point, the real power comes from understanding the *nature* of THOUGHT.

- 4th wave (THOUGHT revolution) understanding of the nature of THOUGHT.

The experience economy

There are already numerous signs that we're moving towards an "experience economy." As people become more time-poor, attention-starved and values-focused, the quality of their *experience* of life becomes more important. As well as wanting to improve the overall quality of their day-to-day experience, people are seeking out pockets of experience, like oases in a desert.

- Starbucks have built a multi-billion-dollar business based on encouraging people to carve 20–30 minutes out of an already busy day so they can sit on a sofa drinking a five-dollar coffee with their name written on the cup. A 20–30 minute experience, repeated daily for millions of people.

- The Apple Store has helped turn Apple into the most profitable company in the world by creating a brilliantly executed in-store experience, and introducing people to exquisitely designed, high-utility "lifestyle products."

- Adventure tourism (adrenalin sports experiences), sacred travel (spiritual hotspots for New Agers), extreme tourism (travel to very dangerous places) and eco-tourism (ecologically friendly travel) are all examples of people's willingness to pay for values-based experiences.

So how does an individual or a business capitalize on the chaos, complexity and uncertainty that the current wave-shift is bringing?

The critical 4th-wave factor

There's one thing that affects the quality of experience a person has more than any other factor…

Your level of clarity; the state of mind you're in when you're having it.

Clarity is "the difference that makes the difference" when it comes to any experience:

- A couple go to a movie. One of them is fully engaged and loves it, the other is bored and distracted. The one who's engaged has a clear mind, the one who's distracted has a head full of boring, distracted thinking.

- Six people are sitting in a business meeting. The difference between a grindingly dull waste of time and a productive, generative experience is the level of clarity of the participants.

- A family go on holiday to the Seychelles. Four of them love it, but the teenage son finds it tedious. Clarity is what makes the difference.

The value of an event is dependent on the quality of the experience the person has. The quality of the experience a person has is 100% dependent on their level of clarity when they're having the experience. This is why understanding the nature of THOUGHT is so fundamental to the experience economy.

As the Information Revolution continues to gobble up people's attention, the critical factor influencing their ability to enjoy any given experience will be their clarity of mind.

So far, in the experience economy, businesses have taken responsibility for managing more and more of the external aspects of a person's experience. Video-game designers have taken it a step further, and are masters of influencing the neural events that their players experience.

Some people argue that the next step isn't the experience economy; that we're now in the "connection economy" or the "creativity economy". They may be correct, and whether they are or not, the leverage points are still the same: clarity of mind and clarity of understanding. The Thought Revolution is already in progress.

The future belongs to those who are willing to go one step further than that, and start influencing their customers' understanding of how life works.

Reality Check

"But wait!" I hear you say. *"If everyone's walking around feeling fulfilled and clear-headed, won't it be like living in a society of zombie bliss-robots? What about my personality, my individuality, my self?"*

There's nothing to worry about. The person who is living from the outside-in misunderstanding is far more robotic (innocently) than a person living from clarity and well-being. As your clarity of understanding continues increasing, you're far more likely to make the difficult decisions, and be guided by your wisdom.

The reality of innate thinking has the power to touch our true identity; our essence; our spirits. And as we continue waking up to who we really are, we discover that the very thing that can make the biggest difference in our own lives also represents our most profound contribution to humanity, the world and to all of life…

keep exploring ⁙ connect with others
share your discoveries ⁙ deepen your understanding

Reflection point: The Industrial Revolution gave rise to a massive, sustained increase in the standard of living for huge numbers of people. This was a step-change unlike anything in humanity's history. Has it occurred to you that we could be on the verge of another, similarly profound step-change?

In fact, the next profound step-change is already in progress. Surf's up! It's an extraordinary time to be alive, and you can be part of the transformation. Get involved! Get over to the additional resources section for this chapter, explore the resources you find there and connect with other people. Every time you do this, it can help you increase your clarity of understanding. Just scan the QR code or use the URL to get in the game now...

www.ClarityBook.biz/chapter22

23

The Art of Sustainable Change

"Culture eats strategy for breakfast."

Peter Drucker,
Management consultant
and writer

"We have developed speed but we have shut ourselves in. Machinery that gives abundance has left us in want. Our knowledge has made us cynical, our cleverness hard and unkind. We think too much and feel too little. More than machinery we need humanity. More than cleverness we need kindness..."

Charlie Chaplin made the arrestingly beautiful final speech from *The Great Dictator* in 1940, but it seems more relevant today than ever. Chaplin's courage, humility and wisdom echo across the intervening years like a prophesy.

Artists like Chaplin are the canaries in humanity's coal mine, able to sense our emerging patterns and potentials long before they become obvious to everyone else. And, while his warnings about our relationship to technology are uncannily prescient, his message of hope for our individual and collective future shines through even more strongly.

The fact is, we have good reason to be optimistic. Your desire for clarity is life evolving through you. The fact that you're reading this book *means* that you are in the process of evolving, whether the external forms of that evolution are already apparent to you or not. As you sit here, reading this, you can relax in the knowledge that the deeper currents of your personal transformation are already moving in, around and through you and your life.

The end of the caterpillar's world

Once a caterpillar sheds its skin to reveal the chrysalis that will offer protection during the process of metamorphosis, something extraordinary happens...

The caterpillar starts to disintegrate!

The digestive juices that used to break down its food now dissolve most of the caterpillar's body, resulting in a kind of "caterpillar soup." This creative broth contains a small number of surviving body parts as well as a huge number of *imaginal cells* that have been contained within the body of the caterpillar since it was born.

The imaginal cells join up to create the tissues and structures of the adult butterfly. The change from caterpillar to butterfly is not an incremental process; the caterpillar doesn't sprout wings. Rather, as the imaginal cells form together around a pre-existing pattern, the butterfly emerges from the caterpillar soup.

The metamorphosis from caterpillar to butterfly can be a compelling metaphor for personal and collective transformation...

- The blueprint of the butterfly already exists within the body of the caterpillar, "contained" in the imaginal cells. Similarly, the pattern of your transformation is already there within you, "contained" within the formless energy of who you really are.

- The caterpillar doesn't "work at" becoming a butterfly; it transforms in harmony with its pre-existing nature. Similarly, you don't have to struggle or "work at" transformation. Aligning to who you really are is in harmony with *your* pre-existing nature.

- The change from caterpillar to butterfly is a metamorphosis; a genuine transformation at the most fundamental level. Similarly, aligning to your most inspired and inspiring life is a genuine transformation; a profound reordering of your experience of life, and how you relate to it.

DISTINCTION: Augmentation vs. Transformation

Augmentation is the process of enhancing, improving or increasing something. Most business training, coaching, and personal development processes are oriented towards problem-solving and goal-setting; helping a person augment their lives and become more "well-adjusted" to living within the context of the outside-in misunderstanding.

> **Transformation** means changing the form or the underlying structure of something. The shift to an insightful understanding of innate thinking is a genuine transformation, changing the underlying structure of how a person relates to and experiences life. From this position, new solutions, goals and directions appear that were invisible from within the "augmentation" mindset.

Every person on the planet has the implicit ability to understand the true nature of life. It's there within each one of us, like the imaginal cells in the body of the caterpillar. As we start waking up to that deeper nature, our experience of life is transformed, and we start to live in a new world.

Paradoxically, as we increase our clarity of understanding, the external form life takes is often "augmented" in ways we never would have predicted from within our old, outside-in misunderstanding. Whatever form it takes, there's a growing sense that you're living a life that fits you perfectly.

A deeper, more profound understanding of life also gives you new eyes. Situations that were once complex and baffling suddenly look much simpler when you can see the principles of innate thinking at work. Problems that seemed impossible to solve often melt away when clarity and wisdom come into play. Frustration can be transformed to understanding, and resentment to compassion as we see that every person is subject to the ups and downs of life, and that we're each using these principles to create a unique, individual experience of reality.

Separate realities

Once we realize that our experience of life is created from the inside-out, it follows that we each live in a unique, THOUGHT-generated experiential reality. No two people live in the same experience of reality, and each person's reality looks real to them (remember; THOUGHT creates the world then says "I didn't do it.")

Almost everyone on the planet today is operating from within the outside-in misunderstanding; very few of us realize the fact of "separate realities." In fact, even when we insightfully understand the inside-out nature of life, it's still surprising how often we get "tricked" into thinking we live in an outside-in world.

But as you continue increasing your clarity of understanding, you become more and more likely to see the "psychological innocence" in yourself and others. Every person is doing their best from within their existing level of understanding. If we had their thinking, we'd be doing the same thing as they are. When our clarity of understanding rises, we act accordingly. As we see more clearly and feel better, we start to do better.

Reality Check

"What about murderous criminals and tyrannical dictators" I hear you ask. *"Are you honestly suggesting they're innocent; that they're not responsible for their crimes?"* Of course they're responsible for the crimes they've committed, and they need to be dealt with accordingly. But they are *psychologically* innocent. As strange as it seems, their misdeeds "made sense" to them from the THOUGHT-generated experiential reality they were living in at the time, misinformed and compounded by the outside-in misunderstanding.

In Semmelweis' day, doctors *innocently* infected patients with dirty scalpels. It was an inevitable result of their level of understanding at the time. As soon as they had a deeper understanding of the nature of germs and bacteria, they acted accordingly, washing their hands and sterilizing their instruments.

Most of humanity's problems at the individual, organizational and global level are the inevitable result of our current level of (mis) understanding. As soon as we have a deeper understanding individually and collectively, we'll act accordingly. As more and more people start seeing through the outside-in misunderstanding, our world will change.

The network effect

The "network effect" describes the impact that one additional user has on the value of a network to all the other users. When only one person had a telephone, it had no value, but as each user was added, the value of the service increased for everyone. The same is true for email, Facebook, Twitter, and all other services that have a networked aspect. As each person is added to the network, *the value of the network increases for each person.*

With a metaphorical leap, you can look at superstitions and new paradigms in a similar way. Today, the vast majority of humanity is operating from the outside-in misunderstanding. By the time a child is six years old, they've been told in 100,000 different ways that they live in an outside-in world. In a world where outside-in is a "fact" for almost everyone, the "network effect" is strong; the outside-in misunderstanding is reinforced wherever we look.

But when you wake up to the inside-out nature of reality, two things happen: the strength of the outside-in network effect reduces and the strength of the inside-out network effect increases. As you wake up to the inside-out nature of life, you make the power of the inside-out understanding stronger for everyone, as well as making it easier for the next person to see it for themselves.

Thought Experiment

London's Wembley stadium holds a staggering 90,000 people. Imagine it, filled to capacity, with each person holding an unlit candle in their hand. Suddenly the lights go out, and the stadium is plunged into darkness. In the midst of the blackout, a single candle is lit. Everyone can see the tiny pinprick of light, and they watch as the light touches the candles of the people standing near it. Those candles flare into life. Now there are 10 candles burning, then 50, then 100! The amount of light from the candles increases, and now you can make out people's faces. Within minutes, 10,000 candles are burning, and light fills the stadium. Then 20,000, then 30,000, and so on...

The moment your candle starts burning, you increase the amount of light available for everyone, and the darkness is further diminished.

The world is changing more rapidly than ever before; old systems are crumbling as new ones emerge to take their place. And while there are more people on the planet than at any point in history, we live at a time when each individual has enormous power to take part in creating our world.

Management guru Peter Drucker famously said that "culture eats strategy for breakfast." Disruptive businesses, from Apple to Zappos, demonstrate the truth of Drucker's assertion. He was implicitly acknowledging that even the most brilliant strategy is reliant on people to implement it; people whose culture (the shared set of stories, values, beliefs, assumptions, understandings and worldviews they live from) means the difference between success and failure.

In her book, *Conscious Evolution*, futurist Barbara Marx Hubbard uses the term "cultural creatives" to describe people who are transforming and waking up to their true nature. Hubbard takes the butterfly metaphor one step further, suggesting that cultural creatives are the imaginal cells in the caterpillar of our civilization, coming together to form the butterfly of our collective future.

If this seems far-fetched, ask yourself this: What would your company be like if everyone who worked with you had an insightful understanding of innate thinking? What would your *world* be like if everyone you *knew* had an insightful understanding of innate thinking? How would they behave if they already felt good in themselves and about themselves? How would they act if they were guided more by wisdom than superstitious thinking? I encourage you to create your own projections of what our world would look like from this new paradigm.

The job of creating a coherent vision for the future of humanity is far beyond the scope of this book. But, while we have some massive challenges facing us, we have good reason to be hopeful...

- Most people on the planet have never been involved in a war.

- The streets of most cities are safer than ever before.

- Medical science is able to treat more conditions than at any time in history.

- The Arab Spring saw global connectivity facilitating the over-throw of some tyrannical regimes.

- Customers are calling for the companies that serve them to be increasingly authentic, transparent and socially responsible.

- Citizens are demanding that the environment be placed at the top of government and corporate agendas.

- Global connectivity means that new ideas spread faster, more effectively and more easily than at any point in history.

It's understandable that people sometimes feel powerless and overwhelmed when confronting the big problems and challenges that face humanity. But there's an even bigger reason to be optimistic. You see, there's an incredible elegance implicit in the truth behind our experience of life. The outside-in superstition means that people are innocently looking outside themselves for something that can only ever come from within. But it doesn't work that way; it only works inside-out. And when we truly hear that for ourselves, we resonate with it.

Stop and consider this for a moment...

Just as the blueprint of your most inspiring,
successful life already exists
within your consciousness,
the blueprint of humanity's most inspiring,
successful possibility exists within our collective consciousness...

Your response to the desire for genuine transformation boils down to a simple decision. Do you choose to...

a) Play an unwinnable game, struggling within the outside-in misunderstanding, or...

b) Focus on increasing your clarity of understanding, aligning with your true nature and living your most inspiring, fulfilling and successful life.

It's worth taking some time to reflect on this choice. Superstitious thinking can be compelling, and we all get tricked by it from time to time but, at the end of the day, it's still just an illusion. When you decide to make it a priority to deepen your understanding of innate thinking, you're aligning yourself more closely with reality, and with your true nature.

This is the essence of clarity.

We are all in this together, each playing our part in the unfolding of life, our personal and collective evolution. The fact that you're reading this book means that you're looking in the right direction; the principles behind innate thinking. Keep looking in this direction, and your clarity of understanding will continue to increase as you enjoy the powerful benefits of insight and realization.

Above all, remember this: we're all human; we all have our ups and downs. We're generating our experience of reality from the inside-out, using the power of THOUGHT. And while we don't get to choose the timescale, new thinking can show up in any moment. And when new thinking arrives, our world changes.

keep exploring ⁙ connect with others
share your discoveries ⁙ deepen your understanding

Reflection point: What if there's a bigger picture here? Many forward-thinking business leaders believe that we're in the midst of a profound societal transformation. Could the fact that you're reading this book mean that you're an integral part of the "societal DNA" for what's to come?

I hope so. It's going to be a lot more fun being part of the butterfly than being part of the cocoon that gets left behind! Get involved, connect with others and share your discoveries; it's one of the most reliable ways to continue deepening your clarity of understanding. And, of course, there are extra resources relating to Chapter 23.

www.ClarityBook.biz/chapter23

24

Inspired Action

....

"Forget safety.
Live where you fear to live.
Destroy your reputation.
Be notorious."

Rumi, Poet

"Inspiration often shows up when you're already doing something else..."

So...

Show up...

Grow a pair...

Get in the game...

Stay in the game...

Step into the unknown...

And keep experimenting...

Pause and reflect from time to time...

Discover your "how" as you take the next step...

Remember, you're living in the feeling of your thinking...

When your wisdom reminds you of this,
relax... The system is self-correcting...

If you find you're pointed in the wrong
direction, adjust as necessary...

Become willing to make mistakes and learn from them...

Keep increasing your clarity of understanding...

You're capable of far more than you think...

Because you are far more than you think...

Discover your path by walking it...

And be grateful for the highs...

Graceful in the lows...

And do your best...

To enjoy yourself...

Every step of the way...

Secure in your increasing understanding...

Of how the system works...

keep exploring ⦂ connect with others
share your discoveries ⦂ deepen your understanding

Reflection point: Enough reflection; it's time for some action. When you get to the extra resources area for this chapter, you'll find a version of the preceding page that you can print out and put up on your wall. There's lots of other good stuff there for you too, as your reward for making it all the way to the end of this book. Thanks for reading Clarity; I look forward to connecting with you in person or via the internet at some point in the future.

www.ClarityBook.biz/chapter24

List of Distinctions

....

Acknowledgments

The author's name is on the cover, but there are always others without whom a book would never see the light of day. Countless people have contributed to me, my learning and my work over the years. I will never be able to fully thank them all. However, there are a number of people whose support and guidance have been integral to the creation of this book. Special thanks go to...

The members of my Inner Circle Group, for coming with me on this journey...

All the wonderful people who have joined my community, read my articles and used my products and services over the years. You've supported me in doing what I love since 1998...

Cathy Casey, Chip Chipman, Garret Kramer, Mark Howard PhD and Sandy Krot for standing by me when the going got tough. I've learned so much from what you've shared with me, and even more from who you are...

Terry Leahy, for your clarity, compassion and peerless guidance...

Keith Blevens PhD and Valda Monroe, for hanging in there and illuminating the single paradigm...

Syd Banks, for sharing what you saw...

Ian, Megs, Andrew and Lindsey (my dad, mum, brother and sister); you can choose your friends, but when it comes to family, it's the luck of the draw. I was born lucky...

Andrew and Lisa, for putting me up (and putting up with me) during my Whistler odyssey...

Jo Nicholls, for your love, support and flawless intuition...

John Wilkes, for keeping it grounded...

Amer, Fas, John and Richard; few men are lucky enough to have a few men like you to call friends...

Jan Chipman, for your love and wisdom...

Decker Cunov, for reacquainting me with connection...

Sháá Wasmund, for believing in me...

Michael Neill, for your love, understanding and support...

Nikki Owen (Managing Director of Jamie Smart Ltd), for keeping the show on the road...

All my teachers, coaches and mentors, (official, unofficial and unintentional). The lessons I've learned from you haven't always been the ones you were teaching, but they've all turned out to be valuable...

And finally, to the phenomenal team at Capstone for believing in *Clarity* and turning it round in record time...

The *Innate Thinking®* model offers a revolutionary approach to high performance, resilience and innovation. It recognizes that outstanding leaders in every field profit from the flow-states that a clear mind brings.

With clarity of mind comes the qualities that drive sustainable results, including leadership, engagement, creativity and intuition. These qualities (and the results they bring) are what individuals and organizations are searching for, but they've been looking in the wrong place until now.

Traditional approaches to coaching, training and organizational change are grounded in *application-based learning*; teaching techniques, skills and methods, then encouraging people to implement them. While these approaches can be useful for routine mechanical processes, their effectiveness drops off sharply for complex cognitive and creative skill-sets. Why?

Because successful implementation depends on clarity, and the qualities it brings.

The *Innate Thinking®* model is grounded in *Implication-based Learning™*, focusing on the foundational principles that drive high-performance. With this approach, there is no separate implementation-step. As individuals see the *implications* of these foundational principles, *implementation* is automatic. Here are some of the key differences between *Innate Thinking®* and more traditional approaches:

Traditional Approaches (application-based learning)	Innate Thinking® (Implication-based Learning™)
• Give people more to think about	• Clears the mind
• Focus on trying to generate effects	• Focuses on leveraging causes
• Separate implementation phase	• Seamless implementation
• Rely on motivation and self-belief	• Drives motivation and self-belief
• Reinforce dependance mindset	• Encourages personal responsibility
• Assume high performance	• Activates high performance

Jamie Smart is dedicated to providing the highest quality of *Innate Thinking®* training, coaching and consulting services, in the form of professional development and corporate programmes.

Professional development programmes

The professional development programmes are ideal for coaches, trainers and consultants who want to leverage the principles of *Innate Thinking®* in their work with clients. These programmes are also an excellent fit for entrepreneurs, business owners and other leaders who want to benefit from an understanding of *Innate Thinking®*. They include...

- *Innate Thinking®* Discovery Programmes

- The *Innate Thinking®* Licensed Practitioner Programme

- The *Innate Thinking®* Licensed Consultant Programme

- Life Transformation Coaching, Retreats and Intensives

These programmes can also be run on an 'in-house' basis for larger organizations. You can find programme details at
www.JamieSmart.com/professional

Corporate programmes

Jamie Smart and his team of highly-skilled *Innate Thinking*® consultants work with individuals and businesses to unlock resources and deliver bottom-line benefits. Areas where an understanding of *Innate Thinking*® is particularly relevant and impactful include...

- Leadership
- Team-building/team-alignment
- Strategy and vision
- Performance enhancement
- Resilience
- Creativity and innovation
- Intuition and decision-making
- Listening and communication
- Persuasion and influence
- Relationship-building
- Employee engagement
- Conflict resolution
- Problem-solving
- Coaching skills
- Culture change
- Project recovery

If you want to explore the possibility of Jamie and his team working with your organization, contact us using one of the methods below. You can find more details at **www.JamieSmart.com/corporate**

You can connect with Jamie Smart using the following methods	
Twitter:	@Jamie_Smart_
LinkedIn:	http://www.linkedin.com/in/JamieSmartClarity
Email:	clarity@JamieSmart.com
Website:	www.JamieSmart.com
Phone:	+44 (0) 333 444 1982
Address:	Jamie Smart Ltd Unit 4B 43 Berkeley Square Mayfair London W1J 5FJ

Jamie Smart [Ⓙ]

....

Jamie Smart is an internationally renowned writer, speaker, coach and consultant. He shows individuals and organizations the unexpected keys to clarity; the ultimate leverage point for creating more time, better decisions and meaningful results.

Jamie is a gifted speaker, equally engaging in front of large audiences and more intimate groups. He's passionate about helping individuals and businesses to deepen their understanding of *Innate Thinking*® and to create the results that matter to them. In addition to working with a handful of coaching clients and leading selected corporate programmes, Jamie runs professional development workshops for business leaders, trainers, coaches and consultants. He has appeared on Sky TV and on the BBC, as well as in numerous publications.

In 2003, Jamie started the company *Salad*, quickly growing a tribe of over 80,000 people who devoured his articles and personal development products. *Salad* soon became the world's leading NLP product business, and he was acknowledged by his peers as one of the world's finest trainers. Then, in 2008, Jamie shifted his focus to a new paradigm, the principles of *Innate Thinking*®. He stopped teaching NLP and in 2012, sold *Salad*.

Prior to starting *Salad*, Jamie led multi-million pound organizational change programmes and was also brought in as a troubleshooter to rescue struggling projects. His client list includes the *Guardian* newspaper, Sweet & Maxwell, Payzone and Dun & Bradstreet.

Jamie lives in London. When he's not working, he loves travelling, walking, drinking coffee and exploring.

For more details about Jamie's corporate and professional development services, as well as full contact details, see the previous *Innate Thinking*® section.

You can read Jamie's blog at **www.JamieSmart.com** and connect with him on twitter here: @Jamie_Smart_

www.JamieSmart.com

Index